BEYOND THE LIMIT

BEYOND THE LIMIT

SID WATKINS

Foreword by Jackie Stewart

MACMILLAN

First published 2001 by Macmillan
an imprint of Macmillan Publishers Ltd
25 Eccleston Place, London SW1W 9NF
Basingstoke and Oxford
Associated companies throughout the world
www.macmillan.com

ISBN 0 333 90188 6

1 3 5 7 9 8 6 4 2

A CIP catalogue record for this book is available from
the British Library.

Typeset by SetSystems Ltd, Saffron Walden, Essex
Printed and bound in Great Britain by
Mackays of Chatham plc, Chatham, Kent

To the drivers of the FIA Medical Car who have conducted me safely round circuits worldwide, sometimes in appalling conditions and sometimes in appalling cars. Nevertheless, for the countless first laps, the many re-starts and the accidents to which I have been taken, I am grateful to have arrived in good condition. Over the years – and over 300 Grands Prix – there have been so many drivers of so many nationalities who have shouldered the responsibility of not screwing up the first lap that I cannot name them all. But I would like to say a special thank you to Alex Ribeiro and Frank Gardner who have driven me more than any other drivers and probably quicker than any others.

CONTENTS

CONTENTS

ACKNOWLEDGEMENTS

I would like to thank Max Mosley, President of the Fédération Internationale de l'Automobile, for his graceful permission to publish the data from the research activities of the FIA contained in Appendix 1 and similarly for the changes in the regulations to increase safety enforced by the FIA in Appendix 2, and for the Formula One Injury Statistics in Appendix 3. I would like publicly to record my thanks to him for his unlimited support of the work of the Research, Safety and Medical Commissions of the FIA, and for his personal support of my efforts as President of these Commissions. My thanks go also to Bernie Ecclestone, not only for his intense drive and support of my efforts, but also for his humour and the need for continuing vigilance to protect myself from his leg-pulling.

I am most grateful to Nigel Roebuck for accepting the onerous task of reading the text of the book and for his corrections of my inaccuracies. I much admire him as a writer and I hope his experience of reading my attempts were not too painful or boring.

Apart from memory, I have relied very heavily on Jacques Deschenaux's *Marlboro Grand Prix Guide (1950–1999)*, and on a splendid book I found in a secondhand bookshop in Chipping Camden for £5 called *The Grand Prix Drivers* by Hazleton Publishing, edited by Steve Small and published in 1987. I have had great pleasure re-reading Innes Ireland's two books, *All Arms and Elbows* and *Grand Prix Driving Today. Autosport* and the Grand Prix reports were fundamental for information, as was *Autosport*'s *Grand Prix Review 2000.*

I thank Lynne Sharpe and Roslyn Osinski for typing the manuscript. I thank Peter Wright of the FIA for technical help and for the definition of Units in Appendix 1, and Hubert Gramling of Mercedez Benz, Andrew Mellor and Brian Chi of the Transport Research Laboratory for all their help over the years.

Finally, I would like to thank Georgina Morley, Editorial Director at Macmillan, for allowing me to do another book, and Hazel Orme, my copy editor, for her diligence in keeping me to the straight and narrow. Any other cock-ups are my own responsibility.

FOREWORD

Sid Watkins' new book paints graphic pictures of many of the people in Formula One Grand Prix racing. It also contains a great deal of humour. As in *Life at the Limit*, there are many behind the scenes tales of his untiring efforts constantly to improve the standards of safety in motor sport, efforts that benefit competitors in all categories. I worked very hard in my time in racing and I know how difficult a job it is to talk people into making improvements, not only to save life and prevent serious injury, but also to avoid the sort of accidents that – in a great many cases – should never have occurred. Sid Watkins is a glowing example to everyone in the sport of how to go about your business while retaining the respect and love of so many.

Sid is a remarkable man, with whom I have been friends for over twenty years. I have always been ready to support his cause for greater safety. He has taken on some pretty big challenges, sometimes against the institution and the very people who appointed him to his job but they, like me, respect him. He knows where to exert pressure and how to get his way. Sid is also a man who is available to everybody in the paddock in times of trouble, accident, injury or illness.

He is totally reliable, with a wicked sense of humour and this sense of fun comes shining through in his book.

Sid Watkins has earned his place at the highest levels of respect and integrity within the sport and, if he ever gets tired of medicine, the speaking tour circuit would be a worthy alternative for his dry, often sarcastic wit and good clean humour.

Jackie Stewart, OBE
January 2001

INTRODUCTION

In October 1994 I started to write a book triggered by sadness at the loss of my good friend Ayrton Senna on 1 May 1994 at Imola. I was in Jerez de la Frontera recalling another horrible accident in which Martin Donnelly nearly lost his life. *Life at the Limit* was about the triumph and tragedy of Formula One racing, and it detailed the struggle I, and others, had to reach a high standard of medical safety at the circuits. It also had its share of behind the scenes stories about some of the sport's most remarkable characters.

It is seven years since Roland Ratzenberger and Ayrton Senna died. In the years since then there have been many changes, changes which were triggered by the tragedies at Imola. Not the least among these is the attitudinal response to any injury in motor racing at Grand Prix level as shown by the response to the accidents of Oliver Panis and Michael Schumacher in 1997 and 1999 respectively. Max Mosley, President of the FIA, has since launched a zero option policy with the goal of zero mortality in the sport. Much research and development has gone towards the technical changes in the car, circuit design, safety, barrier development and personal protection in the cockpit. But this growing edge of research into the prevention of injury by study of the biophysics of accidents will always be accompanied by uncertainty. The unpredictable nature of events is inherent in the sport and provides the excitement and thrill for the drivers and their audience but also its dangers.

This new book relates the significant incidents between 1994 and 2000. There is also a race-by-race account of the millennium season, with some memories of my own life at the circuits and my views of the current F1 drivers. Finally, there are some happy memories of some of F1's golden oldies.

It becomes apparent in the Appendices which outline the continuing search for safety, and the statistics of injury, that the young men of Grand Prix racing are subjected to stresses far beyond previously accepted levels of human tolerance. In these circumstances it is fair and just to entitle this book *Beyond the Limit*.

Sid Watkins
Paris, France
10 January 2001

■▼■▼■▼■▼■▼■▼■▼■▼■▼■▼■▼■▼■▼■▼■▼■

PART ONE

THE YEARS BETWEEN

1996

Melbourne: March

I guess the outstanding event at the beginning of 1996, before the season started, was Mika Hakkinen's recovery from the devastating accident he suffered in Adelaide the previous year. After an initial period in hospital in Adelaide he came to London where it was necessary for him to undergo surgery as the accident had affected his hearing. Of course, he was a big hit with the nursing staff, who enjoyed having him around, particularly as he was quite well in himself and full of fun.

We all went off to Melbourne for the Australian Grand Prix, the first race of the season, which was also the first race to be held in Albert Park. There had been a good deal of protest about using the picturesque park as a race circuit. Just before the race, despite tight security, a bomb threat was received. The circuit people thought that whoever wanted to set it off was going to do so at the beginning of the first lap, provoking worry that it might actually disrupt the start. Bernie Ecclestone, with his usual sense of humour, said, 'Well, if we have to have two starts, that's more fun, so that's OK.' In fact, nothing happened, but the first lap was somewhat explosive anyway.

3

With the great Australian race driver, Frank Gardner, driving me in the medical car as usual, we set off behind the pack. There were several large outside TV screens around the circuit and as we flashed past one I saw that one of the Grand Prix cars a couple of corners ahead of us was high in the air. When we arrived at the scene we found that it was Martin Brundle's Jordan. By then, he was out of the car, which was completely inverted and largely destroyed. Martin put his thumb up when he saw my car arrive. As he had one of the Australian doctors with him and it was clear that he was OK, I said to Frank, 'Off we go again.' However, the race had been red-flagged so we went gently round to the back of the grid to wait for another parade lap before the second start. Frank and I were sitting in the car when we saw Brundle running towards us. I found out later that Eddie Jordan had told him he should get my OK before he could drive again, but we had heard already from the Australian medical team that he was fine.

I got out of the car and saw straight away that he looked as fit as a fiddle, so I said to him, 'Well, do you want to race?' and he said, 'Yes, please.'

'Well, I think you're OK,' I replied, and put my arm around him and gave him a bit of a cuddle – that picture went out on TV worldwide. As he ran back to the pit lane he got a huge round of applause for his courage. We made the second start. There was no problem on the first lap this time and the race settled down.

It was, of course, Jacques Villeneuve's first Grand Prix race, and his form in the Williams had been devastating all weekend. He and Damon Hill were away at the front and there was a good deal of competition between the two of them. Jacques had put his car on pole, with Damon alongside him, and that remained the position in the race for a considerable time until a mechanical problem intervened. Hill won, with Villeneuve second.

After the race I went to the Jordan pit to look at Martin's car, or at least the remnants of it. The survival cell had remained intact and was more or less on its own, with a lot of debris around it. I then saw the tape of the flying accident; it had clearly been a massive shunt. At one stage Martin's car was in the air just above Johnny Herbert's head – Johnny had seen the whole of the vehicle's under-belly before it overtook him to land in the gravel. When the press asked him what it had been like, Johnny replied, 'Have you seen *Top Gun*?'

In April 1995 the racing circus had returned to Argentina for the first time since the Falklands War. I was impressed by the changes in attitude and in facilities that had taken place since the last time I had been there in 1981. The circuit, of course, had been much changed and the Medical Centre, although it was in the same building, had been revamped with a totally new team of medical staff. Now, in 1996, the Williams team were out in front and did a one–two again, as they had in Melbourne. For Damon it was his third Grand Prix triumph in a row as he had won the race in São Paulo a week earlier.

When we had left São Paulo I took the opportunity of visiting the Iguazu Falls. I had been to this remarkable place when we first went to Argentina in the seventies, and had met James Bond there in the shape of Roger Moore. This time I was with my son Alistair, who was working with the FIA (Fédération Internationale de l'Automobile) as their Press Delegate, Jean-Jacques Isserman, the FIA Medical Inspector,

5

and Peter Byles, our FIA Anaesthetist, who had once – as related in *Life at the Limit* – impersonated James Hunt. We had a good time, which included a terrifying ride in a rubber dinghy into the maelstrom of the falls, in particular the Garganta del Diablo, the most terrifying of all the three hundred odd falls. Of course, we all got thoroughly wet and it was with relief that I climbed out of the craft, my nerves shattered.

It was at the beginning of 1996 that we introduced new head-and-neck protection for drivers in the form of a horse-shoe-shaped collar of foam, known as Confor. The research work that had been done at the Motor Industry Research Association at Nuneaton in Warwickshire had shown that 7.5 centimetres of Confor foam covered with a Kevlar skin in the shape of a U, mounted on top of a car's chassis, was extremely protective when tested with instrumented Hybrid III dummies, in that it reduced the G-forces to the head and also the Head Injury Criterion or 'HIC'. The energy-absorbing properties of this foam really had cut down the effects of impact on the head and neck in a most remarkable fashion. In fact, it had been one of the several factors which had protected Martin Brundle from serious injury in Melbourne. Many teams had resisted the introduction of this safety device (made mandatory at the beginning of the 1996 season) although it was clear from the research work that it should be introduced. All of the teams, save Ferrari, gave me, as the Chairman of the Advisory Expert Group, a lot of stick because they did not want to introduce the high sides to the cockpits of the cars on the grounds of cost and aerodynamic loss. In fact, one of the team principals came to me, and declared that I had cost him a million pounds because he would have to redesign his chassis. I told him that he could subtract it from the salary of his driver, who was earning seven times that amount of money and probably would not miss a million. Nevertheless, Max Mosley, President of the FIA, stood firm and, despite all the complaints, it was now in all the cars and starting to do its job.

In August 1996, where the Spa circuit sweeps down towards the Medical Centre to the last right-hander, Jos Verstappen had a huge accident: his car went into the barrier at about 100 m.p.h. and it was to everybody's astonishment that he stepped out unaided, albeit somewhat unsteadily and looking a little stunned. The medical staff nearest came to his rescue and helped him into an ambulance. An accident replication performed later at the Transport Research Laboratories in Surrey discovered that the G-forces operating in the accident would have undoubtedly either killed him or caused a major brain injury, without the energy absorption of his crash helmet and the new head-and-neck protection.

The Williams team remained dominant for the rest of the season: after Damon's win in Argentina, Villeneuve won the next race at Nürburgring, then Hill won at Imola, Canada, France, Germany and Japan, to take the world championship. Villeneuve went on to win at Silverstone, Hungary and Portugal and took second place.

Earlier in the year I had been told that I was to receive the Mario Andretti award for excellence in medicine, so on the way to Canada I went to Detroit, where there was a CART race. I was honoured to receive the award from Mario himself and we had a delightful dinner with him and his colleagues afterwards to celebrate.

1997

Montreal: June

We had seen the accident on the widescreen TV close to our car at the pit exit of the circuit on the Isle Notre Dame. Olivier Panis's car had gone off heavily into the wall, rebounded and ended up on the opposite side of the track among the tyres. Whenever high-speed impact like that occurs I watch anxiously to see if the driver is moving. Often, for a few seconds, the helmet remains absolutely still but it always seems much longer than just a few seconds. Sure enough, Olivier's head moved and he made an attempt to get out of the cockpit, but fell back abruptly and gestured for help to two marshals. As this happened I heard Herbie Blash, Assistant Race Director, saying on the radio, 'I think we'd better send Sid to have a look at this.' Immediately we got ready to leave and then came Herbie's instruction: 'Sid, would you please go and have a look at the Panis accident.'

I turned to the medical-car driver and said, 'Let's go.'

To my astonishment, he asked, 'In the middle of the race?'

I realized that perhaps I had not briefed him well enough in the preceding two days. 'Yes,' I said. 'In the race. Let's go.'

His next surprising comment was 'But we don't know where the accident is.'

'If we drive around the circuit we're sure to find it,' I replied, somewhat acidly.

Meanwhile, Herbie had put the safety car on stand-by, then deployed it. The two cars left for the pit exit together, but Oliver Gavin, the safety-car driver, had stopped as we reached the circuit to wait to join the Formula One cars when the leader came round. We went straight out on to the circuit to reach the accident. Panis's car, the Prost, was at right angles across the track, and as I opened my car door to get out a string of F1 cars appeared so I slammed it shut again to give them as much room as possible. Olivier was lying at the edge of the circuit beyond the car and, to FIA anaesthetist Gary Hartstein's and my astonishment, his head and upper torso were inside a roll of bolted tyres – the marshals had put him there for protection – presumably. Gary went to Panis's head and I went to his injuries: it is the normal routine for the anaesthetist to monitor the airway and circulation while I look at the overall situation. Here it was obvious that Olivier's right leg was fractured below the knee, as his right foot and shin were out of line two-thirds of the way down. I reached for my shears to cut open the uniform on the right leg. More help arrived as a large pair of marshal's boots appeared, one of which was perilously close to the site of the fracture. I tapped the boot with my shears to attract the owner's attention and asked him to remove his 'pedal extremities', as Fats Waller called them. I could hear Gary and Olivier talking OK so I got on to examine the damaged leg. The F1 cars were still going past, with Oliver Gavin pacing them in the safety car, and it was pretty noisy. More medical help arrived with splints so I set about splinting Olivier's leg above and below the obvious fracture. Meanwhile the marshals had removed the protective tyre roll, and Gary was putting up an IV (intravenous) infusion. I had a word with Panis about his right leg and he then indicated that his left leg was also painful. I could see no obvious displacement of the shin but there was a bump under the skin over the tibia. The quickest way to deal with this was to splint the left leg to the already splinted right. Once I had done this and Gary had set up the IV we were ready for the ambulance transfer. It was then that I realized there was silence: the race had been stopped.

Olivier went off in the ambulance and Gary went with him. My driver and I drove to the medical centre. Once there Dr Denis's medical team took over with Dr Jacques Buchard in overall charge. The medical team and the medical centre's equipment in Montreal are among the best in the world so I never have any qualms when we are racing at Isle Notre Dame. Alain Prost soon arrived in the centre and we told him that Olivier was OK – one broken leg and, perhaps, two.

The race was stopped fifteen laps before the full distance; 75 per cent of which had been covered. Schumacher won, and I heard later that he had expressed sorrow at Panis's injury and also complained bitterly that it should have occurred at all. I thought this was a bit off – and so, apparently, did Jacques Villeneuve, who said that people frequently broke their legs skiing and implied that it wasn't much to get emotional about. I agreed with this. Panis had had a major accident – the car chassis had snapped across the front of the cockpit in line with the leg fractures – and had had a miraculous escape. I thought we would get some helpful data from this crash but a few weeks later I was disappointed to be told that the accident data recorder had not been working.

That night Olivier had surgery to pin his damaged leg bones; there was considerable soft tissue injury too, for his leg swelled and needed fasciotomy (incisions to release the muscle swelling, thereby preventing muscle death from tension). He took some time to get over all this – and his accident was the first one with serious injury since Hakkinen's 1995 crash in Adelaide.

The year 1997 had started peacefully with a win for Coulthard in Australia then for Villeneuve in Brazil. There was a two-week gap between the races in Brazil and Argentina during which Villeneuve took a holiday. I didn't know that he had any tummy trouble until Sunday morning, when I was summoned to the Williams pit at the circuit in Argentina about an hour before the warm-up. Here I learned that he had had gastroenteritis for four days. He had taken some medication, which had proved ineffective, so he still had the runs. He needed to get this under control before the warm-up began so I advised him to take four Lomotil tablets – twice the normal starting dose. He looked nonplussed, and said, 'What happens if it doesn't work?'

'Well, then we would have to use the champagne cork.'

'How does that work?'

'We stick it up your backside. The higher the pressure gets inside, the tighter the champagne cork gets jammed in the orifice owing to its shape.' He wasn't sure whether or not I was joking but went off anyway to do the half-hour warm-up.

When he came back I asked him how he was and as he had had no more trouble I advised him to come to the medical centre and lie down in the cool and take some fluid by mouth so he wouldn't start the race dehydrated. He asked for an intravenous infusion but we thought this unwise: putting the needle into a vein in his arm might cause a haematoma, which would make it painful for him to drive. As he was on pole position he had a good chance of winning and I didn't want to do anything to destroy that.

About half an hour before the pit lane opened for the cars to circulate for fifteen minutes, I went along with Gary Hartstein and Jean-Jacques Isserman to see Jacques to make sure he was OK. His blood pressure and pulse were fine, he had drunk some liquid and felt better. In fact, he made a very good start in the race and won, despite Montezuma's Revenge.

He went on to have a fabulous year and won in Spain, Silverstone, Hungary, Austria and Luxembourg. He almost won the European Grand Prix, the last race of the season at Jerez de la Frontéra, but an awkward collision between him and Michael Schumacher put paid to that: Villeneuve was trying to drive down the inside of Schumacher at the chicane when Schumacher's car turned in on his. There was an impact and Schumacher's car was left in the gravel, out of the race. Villeneuve was then in the lead but was overtaken on the last lap by the two McLarens who had also swapped places so that Hakkinen was ahead of Coulthard. It was Hakkinen's first Grand Prix win, but Villeneuve took his first world championship.

The collision led to controversy and ultimately an inquiry at which it was deemed that Schumacher had acted wrongly. He was stripped of his second place in the world championship for 1997, and eliminated retrospectively from the results for the whole of that year.

The end of the season brought the retirement of Gerhard Berger. Everyone was sad at this because he was so much fun: his sense of humour and naughty pranks would be missed.

Earlier that summer, he had lost his father, despite which he drove brilliantly at Hockenheim to take first place, and in his last race at Jerez he came fourth, so Gerhard went out on a high note. He continued to work with me in the Expert Advisory Group until his new job with BMW made it impossible for him to attend regularly.

In September I was honoured to receive the Centenary Award of Merit from the Royal Automobile Club which was presented to me in Edinburgh by His Royal Highness Prince Michael of Kent. The award was created to mark the hundreth anniversary of the formation of the RAC. Before the presentation there was a splendid dinner, with excellent company, including my old friend Jeffrey Rose, chairman of the RAC.

At the end of the year, under the auspices of the FIA, a symposium on safety was held in Monaco just before the annual prize-giving at which the FIA's world championships are awarded. Safety experts came from Europe and the United States to represent the major manufacturers and we evolved several research projects to be undertaken in the future.

1998

Melbourne: March

Jacques Villeneuve, the 1997 champion, had become blond towards the end of that year. Now, in Australia, his appearance was a matter of considerable surprise to Frank Gardner, whose sense of humour is as enormous as the continent in which he lives. Frank could not believe his eyes and muttered various unprintable comments about the spectacle of Villeneuve as a blond. As he and I walked to the paddock we spotted, to our astonishment, a blonde lady with exactly the same colour hair and a similar cut. 'There goes Villeneuve with tits,' cracked Frank.

The rest of the weekend was fairly quiet, only notable in that Hakkinen won the race, having switched places with Coulthard who had been leading towards the end of the event. Hakkinen went on to win in Brazil, Spain, Monaco, Austria, Germany, Luxembourg and Japan, and secured his first world championship.

The race in Japan took place almost exactly three years from the time Hakkinen had sustained his big head injury in Adelaide. I was delighted to have seen his gradual progress from when he returned to racing in 1996 until he achieved the potential I always thought he had to become a truly great racing driver.

In 1998 we had our share of massive shunts. In June, in Canada, there was a great tangle at the first corner on the first lap, and at the second start there was a tangle between Alex Wurz and Jean Alesi, but fortunately no one was hurt and there was no need for a third start.

Foul weather, poor visibility and a very slippy circuit in August at Spa caused the most remarkable carnage on the first lap at La Source. We made a normal racing start, despite the conditions – a procedure that seems to be dropping from favour now with the introduction and the more frequent use of the safety car to start a race in adverse weather. In any event Marc Duez was driving the medical car, and we were just behind Ricardo Rosset as we went into La Source. Before you get to the corner it's possible to look across and see, not the circuit but the air above, as it descends steeply to Eau

Rouge. I looked across as usual and saw in the air lots of bits of cars and wheels. I said to Marc, 'There's trouble round the corner,' so he slowed, but Rosset went straight on as if nothing was happening.

We rounded the corner and saw a vast collection of debris – wheels and cars without wings and without their wheels – but mercifully as we drove to the mid-point of the crash scene, nobody seemed particularly hurt. Gary Hartstein jumped out and ran through the back half of the field to make sure everybody was all right while Marc and I drove through to the front to check on everyone there. I think the only casualties were Eddie Irvine, who damaged his elbow, and Rubens Barrichello, who had been struck on the head. There was a red substance on his helmet which he presumed was blood so he thought that he had a head injury. However, upon taking his helmet off it was clear inside and he was unhurt, although he wasn't feeling too sharp. The red was probably paint from the tyre barriers.

It took a considerable time to clear up the mess; it was remarkable that no sizeable piece of debris had gone into the spectators. One man who was in the back of the stand had been struck on the chest by the logo off the Stewart car, which he returned to Jackie Stewart.

After the re-start, the race was pretty exciting, and notable for the remarkable accident that Michael Schumacher had with David Coulthard when the latter was a lap down: Schumacher came out of the mist behind him and hit the back of his car. Schumacher's car was badly damaged and although he got it back to the pit he could not continue in the race. As a result Damon Hill won his first Grand Prix for the Jordan team so there was jubilation among the British.

Marc Duez deserved full marks for driving in very bad conditions in two starts, performing quite brilliantly on both occasions.

In the lead-up to the race Jacques Villeneuve and Mika Salo had enormous shunts in practice. Jacques had clipped the kerb at the bottom of Eau Rouge, arrived at the top out of shape at 180 m.p.h., went into the gravel and hit the barriers. Mika spun out of control at the top of Eau Rouge, and his Arrows car went hard into the tyre barriers. Red paint on his helmet indicated that it had been in contact with the tyre barrier and he had a severe headache. The head-and-neck protection in both cars had been destroyed in both crashes, which indicated how well the deformation of the new device was working.

Salo was sent by helicopter for a brain scan. He came back with it an hour or so later. In the medical centre I showed him the films which image only the bone. I asked him what he thought of his X-rays. 'There's nothing inside the skull,' he said, with some surprise. I told him that that was quite normal for a racing driver, then took him with his X-rays to show his boss Tom Walkinshaw and played the same trick. Tom just looked at me and said, 'Well, what else would you expect?'

We had a great deal of fun at Barcelona in the Spanish Grand Prix. The local man who had been selected to drive the medical car didn't seem up to the task and I thought it would be too dangerous to try to follow the first lap of the Formula 3000 race with this particular gentleman at the wheel. As Niki Lauda was in the paddock I asked him if he would be prepared to drive me. He agreed immediately, asked what time he should turn up, and did as requested just

16

ten minutes before the pit exit opened for the F3000 cars. He climbed into the driver's seat and asked if he could do a lap as he had never driven on that circuit before, nor had he driven the Mercedes 500 Estate Car. I agreed and off we went for a lap during which he drove very fast indeed for someone who had not driven the circuit or the car before. When the race began he drove magnificently, but refused to fasten his safety-belt or wear a crash helmet. When I asked him why he replied, very simply, 'I don't want to be over-confident.'

1999

Silverstone: July

It had been a quiet weekend so far and we had not been out in the medical car to any incident. A huge crowd was enjoying the fine weather as the Formula One cars took off on the parade lap. Alex Ribeiro drove the medical car, with me beside him, on to the tarmac alongside the Brooklyns and Luffield complex and began to warm up the tyres of the Mercedes E estate car. Phil Rayner, our anaesthetist, was in the back. The cars came round, with Mika Hakkinen leading and Michael Schumacher behind him. We latched on to the back markers and followed round Luffield to the start.

Two cars stalled on the grid as the red lights went out, too late to abort the start, and we all took off. Alex dodged the stalled vehicles expertly and took the car into and through Copse corner as quickly as he could. We hammered down to Maggots corner, the F1 cars had strung out and were disappearing into the distance.

When we got to Hangar straight we could see yellow flags waving, and we soon spotted the rear end of a Ferrari sticking out of the tyre wall at Stowe. As we pulled up, Herbie Blash asked over the radio from Race Control if we were going to stop to see to Michael Schumacher. I replied that we already had. It's a long haul over the gravel bed from the tarmac, but we were at Schumacher's Ferrari within eighty-six seconds of the impact. The nearest doctor to Stowe corner was already with the car, and a rescue team was arriving.

As I approached the Ferrari I could see the back of Michael Schumacher's head. He immediately spotted me and said, 'Sid, it's only a broken leg.' The marshals were trying to lift him out, although he had made an attempt to get out himself until he realized his leg was broken. It was a difficult manoeuvre – the broken limb had to be passed round the steering column, but soon Michael was resting on the gravel. Cool as a cucumber, he said, quite dispassionately, 'Sid, can you do two things for me? Phone my wife and tell her it's just a broken leg, then get hold of Jean Todt and tell him to check the other car as it was a brake failure.'

'OK,' I agreed, and we got on with the job of splinting his right leg then strapping both legs together. He took some Entonox – a gas and oxygen inhalant – but didn't like it so politely asked the doctors to take it away. We put him on a stretcher and carried him to the waiting ambulance. The marshals had screens around the scene, but Michael wanted the world to know he was OK so he held his hand above the screens and waved.

While Phil and I were working with the other doctors and rescue crew, Alex Ribero was quietly collecting the head-and-neck protection, which was fractured, Michael's helmet, and the steering-wheel and column, which had collapsed. Later it was found that the monocoque had fractured transversely and that one of the wheels had come right round to the cockpit side.

In the medical centre, my old friend and neurosurgical colleague Brian Simpson took charge and we cut Michael's uniform off him so that he could be completely examined. (Later in the year he accused me of trying to cut off his scrotum, too, and I'm not sure he was joking. In any event I denied having done so on the grounds that I hadn't thought of it but maybe I had got a bit close.) After we had got him organized in the medical centre he asked for a mobile phone so that he could call his wife. By then Jean Todt had turned up in the medical centre and there was nothing more for me to do. I left Michael in the safe hands of the Silverstone Medical Team, and Phil and I pushed off with Alex back to the car for the re-start.

I had noticed the absence of the noise of Formula One engines at the scene of the accident and assumed that the race had been red-flagged because of the crash. As it turned out it had been stopped because of the two stalled cars on the grid, which couldn't be moved before the leaders arrived to start their second lap.

While we were waiting for the re-start, Bernie Ecclestone asked on the radio about Schumacher. I told him the good news in Michael's words – it was only a broken leg.

The re-start and the rest of the race went without event for us, and David Coulthard celebrated his first British Grand Prix win.

Shortly after the race re-started, Michael had gone off in

the medical helicopter to Northampton General Hospital where it was decided by the orthopaedic specialist that an operation was necessary. By the time we left the circuit he was in surgery so there was no point in my going to the hospital.

In Paris a few days later my mobile phone rang. It was Michael to say thanks for the help at the accident and to say how much he had hated the Entonox.

As everyone knows, less than two months after his accident he attempted to practise at Monza but had to give up because of pain. Wisely he delayed his return until the race in Malaysia where he was examined to be sure he was fully fit by Jean-Jacques Isserman, Dr Mohd Zin Bin Bidin, the Chief Medical Officer at the circuit, and me. The media made much of asking what tests he would undergo to determine whether or not he was fit enough to drive. As a former goalkeeper in my school first team, I replied – tongue in cheek – that he would have to take a penalty and score a goal past me. This was a reference to Schumacher's skill as a footballer and goal-scorer. In fact, he had to pass the standard test to get himself out of the car and put the steering-wheel back on in ten seconds. Then we got him to hop about on the limb that had been broken to be sure he was pain-free. In qualifying practice he put his car on pole and in the race ran second to Eddie Irvine, protecting him from the McLaren assault. In Japan two weeks later, he put his car on pole again and was second to Mika Hakkinen, who clinched his second world championship by beating Eddie Irvine by two points. It was clear that Schumacher's accident had not affected him psychologically.

Since the end of 1999 Schumacher has been working with the research group of the FIA in place of Gerhard Berger and has already made many contributions at our meetings for the improvement of safety.

1999 saw a spate of accidents, some extraordinary and all educational. In April, in Brazil, Ricardo Zonta hit the barrier with considerable impact and a metal component penetrated the cockpit in two places, one beneath his buttock, but never quite reached his tender parts. The other penetrated his left foot, slightly damaging the tendons that lift the toes. He had surgery to repair them, and, two months later, when he thought he was fit enough, he came to Monaco where Jean-Jacques Isserman and I examined him with Dr Scarlot, the Chief Medical Officer there. It was clear that Zonta was not yet fit to return: he could not hop on the injured limb and was still unable to extend his foot properly from the ground. We told him he needed more time to recover.

While Zonta was unable to race the seat in the BAR team was occupied by Miko Salo. Some elements in the media could not understand why Zonta was not allowed to return to the car and felt that there had to be some sinister reason for this. I was even accused, or so I was told, of being paid by Salo to keep Zonta out of the car. When one of the suspicious journalists saw me in the paddock at Barcelona, and raised the issue, I turned to Pasquale Lattenedo, Bernie's right-hand man, who was standing alongside me. 'Pasquale, where did you put the money that we get from Salo for keeping Zonta out of the car?'

Quick as a flash, he replied, 'Well, Professore, it's in the usual place.'

The journalist went off, sufficiently bemused not to print the story.

In June, towards the end of the race in Montreal and

watching the same big screen on which we had seen Olivier Panis's accident, we saw Heinz-Harald Frentzen go off in a big way. He had hit a corner in the early part of the circuit where Jean-Pierre Jabouille had had a big accident in 1979. There is not much run-off space there and his car had rotated and was alongside the barrier pointing in the wrong direction. He didn't attempt to get out of it immediately so Herbie Blash asked for the safety car and the medical car to leave. We shot off in the usual way, while Oliver Gavin in the safety car waited to slot himself in in front of the leader. Just before the point on the circuit where Frentzen's car was, there is a small run-off road, so, when we reached it, I asked Alex to park the car so it was right out of the way and off the track. Gary Hartstein and I jumped out and went to Frentzen. When we got there he was banging his fist against the front of the cockpit, shouting, 'Bloody FIA, bloody FIA.' He was upset because he'd had a brake-disc failure, and apparently the brake-disc size had been reduced by an FIA regulation: in his view this had led to overheating and consequent explosion of his right front disc. Apart from being in a thoroughly bad temper he seemed absolutely OK, although he said his legs hurt a bit, particularly around the knees. By then the safety car had the race under control so when a suitable interval appeared we helped Frentzen out of the cockpit, and walked him to the medical car. He climbed into the back with Gary and we sat there quietly until the race finished.

Suddenly I heard Frentzen say, 'I am back now.' As far as we were aware he hadn't been unconscious but, as happens so often after a head injury, the patient may appear intact to an external observer while having a lapse of full consciousness. It appeared that this was so in Frentzen's case.

Later we heard that Frentzen had had a brain scan, which showed an adequate amount of cerebral tissue, and leg X-rays gave no evidence of any fracture. However, Frentzen told me subsequently that the magnet scan had shown some micro-fractures in his knees where he had banged them together and on the side of the chassis. In an attempt to prevent that sort of accident occurring again we have instituted a new safety regulation that the inside of the cockpit must be padded with energy-absorbing foam to protect the legs.

Later that year at Nürburgring there was a multiple shunt at the first corner on the first lap. I saw Damon Hill go off on the left among several other cars, but on the right in the gravel was an inverted Sauber car. Alex drove the medical car as near to it as possible. 'It's Diniz,' he said. Gary and I jumped out and headed for the stricken vehicle. As we did so, I saw a hand projecting from the cockpit just above the level of the gravel with the thumb up, indicating that the driver was OK. To reinforce this message he wiggled it. Now, it takes concentration when you are upside down in a car in the gravel to realise that when you put your arm out you must rotate it so that the thumb is up, pointing away from the ground, when naturally it would point down. But, amazingly, some racing car drivers are more intelligent than one would think.

I knelt beside the cockpit and scooped away the gravel so that I could see Diniz. His visor was open and he said, 'I'm OK.' I told him we were going to rotate the car into its normal position, which we did very gently with the extrication team and the marshals who had arrived at the scene very rapidly. We got it on to its side, with me supporting Diniz's head and neck, then gently lowered it so that it was the right

23

way up. Alex took out the head-and-neck protection and while we supported Diniz's neck his crash helmet was taken off and a neck splint fitted. He was looking quite chirpy and seemed fine so we brought a stretcher alongside and the team extricated him gently without using the extrication seat.

As we laid him on the stretcher he said to me, 'Sid, would you wave and stick your thumb up because my father will be watching on television and it will tell him that I am OK.' I did as he asked. Then he said to me, 'By the way, will you tell them at the hospital that I broke my C4 vertebral body some years ago so that when they X-ray me they won't think that there is a new fracture?' In the meantime the safety car had come out and the cars were being led by Gavin, at least those of them that were left. We cleared up the place, got back in the medical car and went on the internal route to get back to our normal position at the pit exit where we were able to watch the rest of the race on a TV screen set alongside our car.

1999 was a wonderful year for Mika Hakkinen, and with Schumacher absent, because of his injury, from the British Grand Prix in July until the Malaysian Grand Prix in October, Eddie Irvine had a great opportunity to demonstrate his talent as a driver. Apart from this he has a good talent for wit, which he showed on one occasion with remarkable timing. We were in Hungary at the drivers' briefing and Charlie Whiting, the FIA race director, was going through the usual Sunday morning briefing with the drivers. When he finished talking Salo put up his hand to complain about the pit-exit marshal, whose job is to wave a blue flag if a car is coming down the circuit when another is leaving the pit lane. Salo's gripe was that when he was about to leave the pit exit the pit marshal was not waving his blue flag, or even holding it as he should, because he was picking his nose. There was considerable laughter at this, but when it subsided Eddie Irvine enquired, in that unmistakable accent, 'Did he find what he was looking for?', upon which everybody broke up again.

Villeneuve has a good sense of humour, too. In 1998 he had a big accident at Eau Rouge where he went off at the top of the hill and completely destroyed his car going in to the barrier backwards. We rushed out to pick him up. When he got into the car, I said, 'That was a pretty big accident,' to which he replied, 'Yes, I really enjoyed that.' In 1999 he performed the same trick again but did an even better job on the car. Once more we picked him up, and as he got into the car I said to him, 'Well, you made a better job of it this year than you did last,' to which he replied, 'Yes, that's the best accident I've ever had.' A few minutes later Zonta had an even more spectacular accident at Eau Rouge. Later Villeneuve ruefully declared that Zonta's accident had been bigger than his and he was not too pleased about it.

The year culminated for me in an invitation to the Autosport Awards Dinner where I was asked to present the award for the winning Formula One team, which was McLaren. I returned to my seat, thinking I had done my job for the evening, when I was called back to the stage to be awarded the Gregor Grant Trophy for my contributions to motor sport. I was so surprised that I could only come up with a rather short and inadequate speech of thanks. I seemed to be getting a lot of awards all of a sudden – people must be anticipating my retirement!

PART TWO

THE MILLENNIUM SEASON

AUSTRALIAN GRAND PRIX

The first time the Formula One circus went to Melbourne was in March 1996 when, for the first time, the Australian Grand Prix was the opening race of the season. It has held this place ever since. I missed ending the season in Adelaide to begin with, but have now come to look forward to going to Melbourne and starting the season there instead. An added bonus is that I have some good friends there: David Wallace, a neurosurgeon, who trained with me at the London Hospital, and Jimmy Mercer, a very old pal. We had been at Prescot Grammar School together, and then had both gone on to Liverpool University Medical School. At all Australian Grands Prix, including 1985, Dr David Vissenga, with whom I get on very well, has been the Chief Medical Officer – he and his wife had trained at the London Hospital where I was Professor of Neurosurgery. Frank Gardner does the driving and provides me with a steady supply of jokes. The weather is usually excellent, the circuit facilities, location and appearance very good. Tim Schenken, an ex-Formula One driver, is the Clerk of the Course, very experienced, and very organized. Surrounded by good people, what more could one ask?

This year, of course, we were all expecting the resumption

of the McLaren–Ferrari warfare, and wondering whether Mika Hakkinen would get off to a good start in securing the Driver's World Championship for the third time. There was a good deal of hype too about the twenty-year-old Jenson Button, and whether or not he was as good as he was cracked up to be. The Friday-afternoon practice was interesting for him as he collected a bird in the cockpit – not the usual one he looks for but one of the feathered variety. Saturday-morning practice he crashed, and on Saturday afternoon he managed to get on the back row – actually twenty-first. When it came to the race, we were to start immediately behind him, but things would improve! In the Sunday-morning warm-up he was third fastest, but it is always difficult to gauge what a performance in the warm-up might mean: fuel loads vary and mind games are played in preparation for the real thing.

With regard to the rest of qualifying, the McLarens were quick and on the front row, with Mika Hakkinen on pole and David Coulthard, despite a shunt, alongside. Michael Schumacher and Rubens Barrichello were on the second row, with the two Jordans on row three. The symmetry of team line-ups was broken then by Eddie Irvine, with some hope for Jaguar on seventh place, and Jacques Villeneuve with a sterling effort on the fourth row alongside him. Frank Gardner was in his usual relaxed and humorous mood as we went to the line with Roger Capps, our regular anaesthetist in Australia, (except when he went to the Gulf War) in the back. It was a nice start and the McLarens streaked off. We had no work to do and returned to the pit exit.

Button, however, had shot up to fifteenth by passing five of his fellow competitors on the first lap. He was heading for sixth place and a point, when his car failed with twelve laps to go, but it was enough to silence the critics. The fight at the front ended prematurely with the McLarens' engines failing, Coulthard's after ten laps and Hakkinen's after nineteen. So Schumacher and Barrichello cruised home with ten points and six points, respectively. Ralf Schumacher came in third, and good work by BAR brought in Villeneuve fourth and Zonta sixth, the first points ever for this team at the beginning of their second season in the game. Giancarlo Fisichella, in the Benetton, was fifth. As for the Jaguars, Johnny Herbert went on lap one and Irvine on lap six. In the Constructors' Championship, Ferrari had sixteen points and McLaren none.

We had a nice party after the race at the back of the garages with Karl-Heinz Zimmerman who had managed to organize an Austrian oompahpah band, and had a good supply of red wine. Sunday night the Gardners, the Vissengas and myself had dinner (and wine) as usual – a good time was had by all.

BRAZILIAN GRAND PRIX

I like going to Brazil because of the wonderful people there, although I find São Paulo rather depressing. It is an ugly city, for the most part, with many featureless concrete high-rises sticking up into the sky like gravestones in a cemetery. Interlagos, though, is always fun and the circuit very enjoyable, not only because of its design but because of the music and liveliness of the spectators.

This year I flew down from Florida to the race and was met at the airport by Dr Dino Altman, who has been the backbone of the Brazilian Medical Team at Interlagos since the new circuit was opened in 1990 and was now Chief Medical Officer. Until the 2000 season the CMO had been Dr Renato Duprat, who was the chief of the Golden Cross, a medical rescue organization operating throughout Brazil. He was also responsible for the creation of a wonderful new private hospital – the Duprat Hospital – which was beautifully constructed and extremely well equipped with fine medical staff. A couple of years ago Tomas Rohonyi, an old friend and business associate of Bernie's, asked if I would go by helicopter with him and Renato to visit the new hospital which now was one of those designated for the Grand Prix. Being a decent chap, I readily agreed and on the Thursday afternoon before the race we duly left the circuit by helicopter. We arrived on the pad on top of the hospital and descended to the surgical floor. To my surprise, there were a large number of staff, press and TV people assembled – all there to celebrate the inaugural opening of the 'Sid Watkins surgical floor and operating suite'. I was a bit flabbergasted when after a speech of introduction by Dr Duprat – none of which I understood as it was in Brazilian Portuguese – I was called upon to say a few words in response. After inspecting the rest of their excellent establishment, I was glad to get back to the Hotel Transamerica to take a very large whisky.

This year I was able to avoid such embarrassing events and Dino took me to the circuit on the Thursday afternoon to make sure all was well. There I met Alex Ribeiro, who had just finished an exercise in which both the safety-car driver and the medical-car driver, separated by half a lap of the circuit, practise to determine their own and their cars' limits. The television monitor system which observes and records all the events on the circuit is also tested ready for the first

Formula One practice on Friday morning. Alex was his usual cheerful and serene self.

All was well at the medical centre, which is superbly equipped with ITU beds, X-ray, biochemical laboratory and twin operating theatres. The excellent staff include, apart from the usual surgical and anaesthetic staff, orthopaedists, ophthalmic surgeons, dermatologists and even a urologist, who specializes in the treatment of impotence. He always asks me if I need his help yet! So, as you can see, the atmosphere is jolly.

Alex Ribeiro is the gentlest man I have ever known. He is also a deeply religious Christian who has long been hopeful of mending my ways – so far unsuccessfully. Alex, Bernie and I had dinner together in London in December 1998 to set up Alex's voluntary and honorary offer to drive the medical car everywhere for a year. Bernie asked me later why Alex wanted to do it. I replied, 'Alex wants to convert me to Christianity.' Bernie responded, 'A one-year contract isn't enough. We'd better give him ten years and I'll bet at the end of that Alex will be smoking cigars and drinking whisky and you'll be unchanged.' However, since then Alex has driven the medical car nearly everywhere, although he doesn't come to Australia where I have the maestro, Frank Gardner, and he missed Spa in 1999 as he'd had an accident go-kart racing. He had a minor fracture in his leg but he reappeared with a limp for the next race at Monza. Once behind the wheel of a car, he undergoes a personality change. Like Jekyll and Hyde the gentle chap disappears and like most Formula One racing drivers he turns into a devil incarnate, tough on the car and on himself – despite wearing a crash helmet inscribed, 'Jesus Saves'.

He has driven me faster than anyone else, and at Eau Rouge this year I kept looking back to see if my stomach had got left behind at La Source. He impressed me the first time he drove me at Interlagos, at the turn of the seventies in a car that was not fast enough to make a full lap of the old circuit there. It was decided that we could make it if we took a short-cut from the corner at Descida do Lago to a point on the circuit past Mergulho. The idea was that from Descida do Lago one could see the race cars in the infield and if there was no trouble we could cut across, but if there was any need, we could stay on the circuit to get to an accident. The problem when we practised was the gap in the Armco to re-enter the circuit past Mergulho. It was only a few centimetres wider than the car. The circuit people said they would enlarge it a bit, but on the Sunday morning after the warm-up it was still unchanged. The authorities promised faithfully to deal with it before the race. Of course, we might have known it – on arriving at the gap on the first lap of the race, it was still unchanged. Alex was going as quick as he could and he got the car through at speed. I just shut my eyes and waited for the bang – but it didn't come.

This year, the most surprising event in practice, apart from the performance of the drivers, was the interruption of qualifying practice on Saturday afternoon by billboards falling on to the circuit at the end of the pit straight. Jean Alesi was nearly clobbered by one but only his car was damaged. The other surprise in the qualifying session was the performance of Jenson Button, who was faster than his team-mate Ralf Schumacher. He was quick all weekend although he had never driven at Interlagos before. When asked about the circuit, he replied, 'It's great, I really like the place.'

Each time the Ferraris appeared they were greeted with roars of applause. The local hero Rubens Barrichello was performing there for the first time in the red car; the Brazilian crowd are always loyal to their countrymen, making a great deal of noise with drums and trumpets. The stands on the long straight down to Descido do Lago accorded me the usual compliments each time we went round before and after the practice – Pederast! Adulterer! Mother-abuser! – much to the amusement of Alex and our Greek-Brazilian anaesthetist Dr Demetrios, who kindly translated for me.

Once again, qualifying put the McLarens on the front row, with Mika Hakkinen on pole, and the Ferrari came next, with Michael Schumacher marginally faster than Rubens Barrichello, who lost his best lap due to a falling billboard and a red flag. Giancarlo Fisichella was fifth, and Eddie Irvine did a great job to get the Jaguar on sixth.

Race day was hot and overcast, and the warm-up uneventful. Only twenty cars were running because the Saubers had been withdrawn during practice on safety grounds: both cars had suffered wing failures. Salo's had involved him in a shunt, in which he was unhurt.

After the pit exit closed Alex took the medical car round the circuit to park behind the grid and we waited for the twenty cars to appear. He always gets a big cheer from the crowd along the pit straight as we sit behind the grid awaiting the parade lap. The start was clean, and after a comfortable first lap we settled down at the pit exit where we could see about half of the circuit. Schumacher made short work of Hakkinen's first-lap lead, and Hakkinen ran second until Barrichello went past him. Then, to everyone's disappointment, Barrichello's car failed, followed by Hakkinen's a few laps later. Schumacher, therefore, was able to drive to a second consecutive victory, with David Coulthard second on the tarmac. Later Coulthard was disqualified, after scrutineering, on a technicality: his front wing was mounted too low. He was upset about that, for he had put in a fine drive, although his gear-box was malfunctioning for most of the race. This allowed Fisichella to move into second place from third, and Jenson Button into sixth place from seventh. The latter, therefore, became the youngest driver to score a point in the world championship. The net effect of all this on the Drivers' Championship was Schumacher had 20 points, the McLaren drivers had no points, and in the Constructors' Championship Ferrari had 26 points and McLaren had zero.

When the race was over, we returned to the medical centre, passing a wrecked Jaguar at Bico de Pato, where Eddie Irvine had obviously hit the barrier but fortunately without injury. One of the advantages in Brazil is that the medical team usually goes in and out of the circuit in the medical helicopter, which lands on the lawn at the side of the Hotel Transamerica. That day we changed rapidly, and Alex, Gary Hartstein and I presented ourselves to be flown to the hotel. We had a very competent lady pilot this year – very well turned out in smart uniform – her name was Martha, the same as my daughter. It was the first time I'd ever encountered a lady flying a helicopter.

SAN MARINO GRAND PRIX

Imola lies near a mountainous area to the south-east of Bologna. The old part of the town is charming and boasts one of the best restaurants in Italy, the San Domenico, where high-fliers like to eat. This part of the country is gastronomically well endowed, and one of my favourite eating places is Ristorante Naldi, very close to the Hotel Olympia where we stay. It is near enough to the circuit for us to walk there, which is an enormous advantage on race days. Since Ayrton Senna's death the circuit has been much changed but it is still pretty through Acqua Minerale, Variante Alta and down to Rivazza, a corner which, at the bottom of the hill, is approached at very high speed. Tamburello, the scene of so much action, is now hardly recognizable and the same goes for the Villeneuve sector. Tosa, Piratella and Variante Alta are still fun and the steep descent to Aqua Minerale and the climb out of it still demanding.

For many years, the Chief Medical Officer has been Dr Domenico Salcito, an affable man. He has headed up a strong team, with Dr Giovanni Gordini, a skilled ITU expert from the Maggiore Hospital, and a stable staff of surgeons and anaesthetists, including Tony Fabrizzio, an American-Italian neurosurgeon, who replaced my old friend Franco Servadei. The medical centre has excellent facilities and is positioned close to the tarmac but some distance from the *tifosi*, though the crowd here is not as fevered as in Monza.

Dr Salcito's wife is a fabulous cook, and this year, as has been our custom for many years, we dined with them on Friday night. Their daughter speaks excellent English and acts as our interpreter and guardian.

35

Imola has happy memories for me, as well as tragic ones. In the early days I stayed at Rosa's at La Pergola, in Fontanelica, having been introduced to it by Michael Tee. The group of regulars there included Denis Jenkinson, Nigel Roebuck, Maurice Hamilton, Alan Henry and Tony Jardine. With a bunch like that, there was a lot of ribaldry and wit with Jenks, nicknamed 'the gnome', and Alan Henry, F squared as his nickname goes. With Tony Jardine's impressions of Jackie Stewart, Bernie Ecclestone and others we had a lot of fun. One serious problem there was getting to sleep because once Jenks was away and snoring nobody else stood a chance. The food at Rosa's was also excellent – as it is everywhere around Bologna – and together with libations of wine, they were happy times. The propensity for gaining weight in four days in these parts is high. This year, on the Thursday night, we were taken to San Domenico's (first time ever) by the new Chief Medical Officer, Dr Corbascio. Friday was the Salcito's night. Saturday and Sunday nights were spent at Restaurant Naldi. By Monday morning one's belt has to be more liberally buckled and it's time to get back to a more disciplined way of life.

This year, as usual, Jean-Jacques Isserman was with the medical team, Alex Ribeiro was driving, while Giovanni Gordini and his protégé were our anaesthetic support. The weather at Imola is usually good and so it proved again. Despite the early date in April, the whole weekend was fine and bright. On Friday one of the important events for the weekend was an official press launch of the HANS – Head and Neck Support – device by Max Mosley and Professor Jürgen Hubbert of Mercedes. It protects the head and neck in frontal accidents. Professor Bob Hubbard, of Michigan

State University, designed it originally for use by power-boat racers who, when ejected from their boats, were sustaining dangerously high G-forces in the head and neck. When we first looked at the original HANS, in 1995, it was cumbersome. It consisted of a long yoke fitting on each shoulder with a rear semi-circular collar and a vertical structure mounted on the collar behind the head. To this vertical mounting were attached tapes which were tethered to the helmet. The yoke fitting over the shoulders was held in place by the driver's safety shoulder-harness. The idea was that when a driver was thrown forward in a frontal impact, the shoulder belts load the yoke and the snapping forward of the head and neck is reduced by the tightening of the tethers. The G-forces are reduced by preventing the full excursion of the head and helmet. As the combined weight of head and helmet is usually about six kilograms, the shearing strain on the neck joints and discs (6 x the G-force) is less if the acceleration of the head and neck is controlled and the G-force reduced. It was necessary to prove that the forces induced within the head by such arrest of movement are not increased to the point of injury threshold. The Expert Advisory Group had been pleased with the protection achieved with the Confor foam head-and-neck rest for side impact, rear impact and oblique accidents, but the new HANS was something that would work in frontal crashes.

As everyone knows, the frontal airbag technology has proved elusive at Formula One speeds, it seeming to be impossible to avoid accidental inflation and to achieve rapid enough inflation of the bag. But we already have collapsible steering columns to help in frontal impact.

Gerhard Berger tried the original HANS in 1995 and

1996, in private testing, but found it too cumbersome to use in official practice or when racing. Tests at that time with instrumented dummies and HYGE sled simulations proved that the device worked, but that it needed modification and development. The FIA together with Peter Hodgman of McLaren explored this. We were fortunate to be offered the remarkable Mercedes experimental facilities to conduct the research, design and testing by Hubert Gramling a bioengineer of formidable intelligence. The HANS was made much smaller, lighter, and therefore more practical, and its efficacy established. At Imola the device was shown to the press by Max Mosley and Jürgen Hubbert. Mike Doodson asked why the device could not be used by road car drivers. I told him it could – if the tethers were attached to the skull by boring a few holes in it – otherwise road-car drivers would have to wear crash helmets.

Early practise produced a contest between Mika Hakkinen, Michael Schumacher and David Coulthard but Rubens Barrichello was a bit off the pace and the two Jordans intruded in fourth and fifth. However, come the qualifying, there was a repeat of the struggle between Hakkinen and Schumacher for pole. They ended up on the front row, with Hakkinen on pole and very pleased with himself. Coulthard and Barrichello came next, then Ralf Schumacher in the Williams BMW after a good effort. Button was way back, and ended up eighteenth.

We sit at a very good vantage-spot at Imola on the left-hand side of the circuit where the racing line takes a left–right corner to reach the beginning of the pit straight. Here we can see the pit entry, all of the pit straight, and the Formula One cars come close at this interesting corner. There is always some action there, as drivers miss their line or lock up, so it is one of the best spots for viewing in the season. We wait there for the parade lap to end, then we run on to the circuit and line up behind and between the back markers.

The pack went off without any trouble, though I gathered later that Schumacher had made a bad start and had cut across Coulthard in a rather abrupt manner, letting Barrichello get ahead of Coulthard. Hakkinen led until the second pit stop when, once again, the Ferrari pit strategy worked, and Schumacher took the lead as Hakkinen came out of the pit lane in second place. Thereafter Schumacher drove home, giving him three wins in a row. Hakkinen was second, and Coulthard third, having managed to come out of the pits ahead of Barrichello. At least the McLarens got ten points for the constructors' title, and Hakkinen and Coulthard got their first points of the season, but Schumacher now had thirty points; his nearest rival was Barrichello with nine. Ferrari had thirty-nine points in the Constructors' Championship. Villeneuve put in a great drive, going from ninth to fifth at the start and retaining fifth position at the end. Button and Ralf Schumacher failed to finish, and Eddie Irvine in his Jaguar qualified seventh and finished there.

Part of Barrichello's problem, so it was said, was a broken crotch strap that put him off the pace – but I suppose, if one accepts Graham Hill's theory about the effect of crotch straps, Rubens was in for a better night than his day had been. Graham always claimed a crotch strap had a deleterious effect on the libido.

There was great jubilation from the crowd at the Ferrari win, which is just what you would expect at the circuit which Enzo Ferrari had named for the son he had lost – Dino.

BRITISH GRAND PRIX

This was one of the wettest, windiest and worst weekends that I can recall in motor racing and I hope I never suffer a similar one.

Of course, the problem related to the date: Silverstone's usual mid-July date had been brought forward to April, and coincided with the Easter weekend: Friday practice took place on Good Friday and the race was on Easter Sunday. Everyone worried about the possibility of bad weather, and our plans to have the normal Grand Prix Drivers' Golf Day on the Monday after the event were scuppered. This is a fun day, which has run for several years now to raise money for the British Brain and Spine Foundation. (Fortunately we were able to hold it after the Austrian Grand Prix in July.)

That Friday, as everyone had expected, was miserable. The circuit was lashed with high winds and heavy rain, and everyone was in hiding, including the general public and the usual paddock habituees. Towards the end of the morning after the first practice and before the second, Bernie Ecclestone turned up. I met him as I was coming out of Karl-Heinz Zimmerman's motor-home. 'Sid, what's happening?' he enquired, in his mocking manner.

'Not much, it's a non-event,' I replied.

'What do you mean?'

'Well, with the weather and the conditions on the circuit, everybody's hiding.'

'Well, it's all your fault.'

'Why are you blaming me?'

His reply was typical Bernie. 'You're in charge of every-thing so it's all your fault that this thing looks like a mess.'

I pointed out to him that, in fact, it was all down to his changing the date from what should have been a sunny happy weekend to one in the middle of winter. He took this with his normal good humour, and we parted on our usual cheery terms.

I couldn't help remembering that it actually snowed at Silverstone one Easter weekend on the occasion of a *Daily Express* Trophy Formula One race, and on another occasion it rained so hard that more than twenty cars went off at Stowe. Emerson Fittipaldi won the race – he had been sitting in his car in the pits having his tyres changed when the deluge had taken off the rest of the field. He only had to make one lap before the race was stopped because of the bad weather.

Saturday was much the same and, of course, conditions were deteriorating in the parking fields with the constant heavy rain. We all feared that Sunday was going to be just the same, but I awoke to find some evidence of sunshine so Jean-Jacques Isserman and I set off for the circuit with high hopes. However, when we got there, I discovered, to my horror, that Silverstone was engulfed in thick mist. It was clear that we were going to have a problem about running the warm-up because the medical helicopters would not be operational.

As usual Dr David Cranston, Chief Medical Officer at Silverstone, had made arrangements for the helicopters to stay all weekend but the mist also blanketed Northampton, the John Radcliffe in Oxford and Stoke Mandeville near Princes Risborough. None of the three hospitals could accept any helicopter landings. Normally we used the Northampton

General Hospital for general casualties, the John Radcliffe for head, spinal or chest injuries, and Stoke Mandeville for spinal injuries or burns. It was clear that we could not risk starting the warm-up while these hospitals were unable to accept our helicopters.

Around nine o'clock, it looked as though the circuit was clearing and I could see Copse corner, the first after the pit exit, from the pit lane. As the minutes passed, the circuit improved rapidly. However, at twenty past nine, the hospitals still could not take helicopters, and the team managers were advised by Charlie Whiting, the race director, and Herbie Blash that we would have to postpone the warm-up. At ten o'clock the circuit was clear, but still the hospitals were in mist.

Eventually Charlie Whiting, Herbie Blash and I met with the team managers and I explained the lack of rapid transfer facility to any hospital we would normally use. They said they were prepared to run the warm-up late, and that they did not really need the whole thirty minutes. This surprised me, but one or two managers indicated that they would settle for a couple of laps, sort of introduction or initiation laps. We parted to wait for conditions to improve. At about a quarter past ten, I heard that we could land at Northampton General Hospital. However, a specialist injury could not be taken there.

By now I was under a lot of pressure from Charlie Whiting and Herbie Blash to agree to start but I pointed out that our responsibility to the drivers was such that we could not risk an injury in the current situation. Fortunately, about five minutes later, we heard that Stoke Mandeville and the John Radcliffe were now clear, and we could start the warm-up.

Of course other people were having an awful time trying to get into the circuit: the car parks were waterlogged. Even important people with helicopters could not get in. Among them were Ron Dennis and Norbert Haug, who could not fly from Le Manoir aux Quat'Saisons at Oxford as they normally did, and had come by car then got stuck in the traffic jams surrounding the circuit. Somebody announced on the intercommunication system that Ron Dennis was stuck in traffic, much to everyone's amusement. Another who could not get in was Bernie Ecclestone. When he arrived at about eleven thirty, he found me having a cup of coffee with Karl-Heinz Zimmerman. 'Why on earth did you delay the warm-up?' he asked.

'Well, it was like this, you see. I had to wait for some important people who couldn't get in by helicopter. Ron Dennis and Norbert Haug were stuck in a traffic jam so I delayed it until they arrived.'

Bernie looked at me quizzically. 'Why on earth would you do that?'

'For money as usual,' I said, with a straight face.

He saw I'd been putting him on, and went off laughing.

With the weather so capricious it was perhaps not surprising that during early practice the results were unusual, with Heinz-Harald Frentzen and Eddie Irvine ending up on the front row. Saturday qualifying, however, restored some of the usual order with a Ferrari on pole – Rubens Barrichello's! Frentzen held on to his front-row position and, thereafter, the McLarens took the second row with Mika Hakkinen slightly faster and Michael Schumacher fifth. Button outqualified Ralf Schumacher to take sixth.

The warm-up and race were both run in good conditions.

In the race the two front rows got away in their qualifying order. Michael Schumacher made a bad start and dropped to eighth while Button improved to fifth, where he finished. Barrichello led, with Frentzen second, for a long time, but David Coulthard caught and passed them both before his pit stop. Barrichello led again briefly but then he spun off, thwarting what might have been his first Grand Prix win for Ferrari, and his first Formula One win ever. Coulthard went on to win, with Hakkinen second and Schumacher worked his way up to third. Frentzen ran well for some time in fourth when his gear-box failed. But the McLarens were resurgent with sixteen points for the Constructors' Championship, and some vitally important points for both drivers – Coulthard was now on fourteen, and Hakkinen on twelve. Schumacher, however, had squeezed out another four and was on thirty-four.

At the end of the race at Silverstone, I usually run to my car in my overalls, make a dash to the only bridge over the circuit to the main exit to get out before it all clogs up. On this occasion, I had arranged to meet Dr Hugh Scully, the eminent Canadian surgeon, and Jean-Jacques Isserman, at the latter's car, so we could make a dive for it. This I did, but before we could get to the exit lane the whole place was jammed up. We sat there for an hour before anything moved, and then it took another hour to get to the bridge. There I saw, to my horror, that only one lane of vehicles was going outwards because traffic was being allowed to come into the paddock from the outside over the bridge (including trucks and buses) obstructing and preventing the use of the two-lane bridge as an exit. We finally reached the main exit, which sits on a little road that runs north and south along the west side of Silverstone after two and a half hours of frustration.

There we discovered that all traffic was being turned to the right. We followed the directions of the police, and when we got to the main A road in Silverstone village, all traffic was being turned to the left, to the west. Our hotel was on the east side of the circuit and a little bit south, about a mile away. On the A road, going in the wrong direction out of Silverstone village, we were detoured into country lanes and then had to make a huge diversion to find a road that would lead us back to our hotel.

The situation was indescribably bad. All the cars were covered in mud, and in the parking fields what turf there had been was destroyed with the rain and the wheels. Everyone looked dejected, frustrated and angry, but at last we seemed clear of it and made it back to the hotel. It was only a mile from the circuit but it took four and a half hours to get there.

Later, in the bar, there was a great deal of cynical humour about the Silverstone management and their lack of fore-thought about what might happen at Silverstone over the Easter weekend if it rained or snowed.

SPANISH GRAND PRIX

When I got to the circuit on Thursday afternoon, there was great speculation about whether or not David Coulthard would be able to drive that weekend. A few days earlier, he had been involved in a terrifying plane crash. Within a few hours I had heard about it from Max Mosley's PA, Pat Tozer. I rang Ron Dennis to find out exactly what had happened. He told me that the plane's engine had failed and that it had crashed on attempting to land at Lyon. The front half of the plane had been destroyed and the two pilots killed, but Coulthard, his girlfriend, his dog and his physiotherapist had escaped through the shattered fuselage. All had avoided injury except Coulthard, whose ribs had been damaged in the classic seat-belt injury.

It was arranged that I would see him with the Chief Medical Officer, Professor Nalda, and Jean-Jacques Isserman on the Thursday afternoon before the Friday practice when we would decide what to do. We had made arrangements to see David in the McLaren motor-home so that he did not have to go to the medical centre through the paddock crowd. We found him surprisingly cheerful. Upon clinical examination, although he was tender around the ribs on the right side, it seemed that he would be able to manage.

The next day he got through the practices successfully and, with the help of some anti-inflammatory tablets and some simple analgesics, he was able to carry on. Saturday practice found him in fairly good condition, and he qualified well in fourth place alongside Barrichello, while Schumacher, on pole shared the front row with Hakkinen.

The big drama of the weekend, however, was a multiple car accident in the Formula 3000. It began when a car spun into the gravel then back on to the circuit, to be hit by two other cars, one driven by Nicolas Minassian, the other by Mario Haberfeld, whose car was badly damaged. He was unable to get out and we shot off from our usual position at the pit exit and went all the way round the circuit as the accident had occurred at the beginning of the pit straight. When we arrived, two other drivers who had been involved were out of their cars but Haberfeld was still trapped. His knees had come up in the impact, and were jammed against the front of the cockpit and extremely painful. He was unable to get them back into the cockpit, to straighten them out or to flex and free them.

The car's chassis was crumpled and it was very difficult to examine his legs. With my gloves off, I was able to get my hand under his calves and gradually work my way through, to reach Gary Hartstein's hands and get a strap around Mario's legs below the knees. It seemed to me that he might have fractured his right thigh and his left leg below the knee. We managed to get some ties around the middle of his thighs so his legs were strapped together, but he was in so much pain that we could do little more until we gave him intravenous analgesic and sedative drugs. He was conscious throughout and kept saying to me, 'Dr Sid, get me out.' I explained to him that we were trying to do that with the least discomfort to him, and the least risk to his legs. Gradually, we got his pain under control, but all of this was taking a long time and we were surrounded by unhelpful marshals. Despite the fact that our local anaesthetist from Professor Nalda's team spoke fluent Spanish and was asking for help, they were extremely unresponsive. They brought car-cutting equipment to the scene but it would not cut the carbon-fibre cockpit and merely crushed it.

We decided that the only way to get Haberfeld out was to use the spinal splint. The extrication team, who were well trained, proceeded to put it on to him so that his torso, arms and pelvis were all supported and strapped together. We now had him in one piece, as it were, and after another intravenous analgesic injection I told the team to start to lift him out gently. As his hips unflexed, I could guide his thighs and knees out of the cockpit, very gently and very slowly. Once his knees were straight, I could deliver his trapped legs from the collapsed chassis. They came out eventually and, much to my surprise and pleasure, appeared to be unfractured. He had a large gash in his left thigh but apart from that did not seem as badly injured as I had first thought. We moved him to a deformable mattress, tucked him in and put him into the ambulance. Gary went with him to the medical centre and I set about clearing the site of the accident, then driving the medical car off the circuit to the control tower.

At the medical centre, it seemed that Haberfeld had escaped any obvious fracture of the legs, and Professor Nalda sent him to hospital. However, later that night we heard that the soft-tissue injury had resulted in such massive swelling of his legs that it had been necessary to operate on him to relieve the pressure and the tension in the muscles by making incisions in the skin to allow the muscles to expand and avoid the loss of the blood supply to the limbs – so-called fasciotomy.

The accident taught us some lessons: if Haberfeld had been in one of the new extricable seats that we had designed for Formula One, we could have strapped him into it instead of using the spinal kit. He could then have been taken out of the car much more rapidly. The other thing we learned was that the so-called 'jaws of life' with which the Spanish had tried to cut the chassis were of no use for cutting carbon fibre. At the next research group meeting, we decided that the FIA should develop a standard for the appropriate equipment. Charlie Whiting asked Joe Bauer, our FIA engineer, to look into the equipment that was available and sufficiently portable to be carried in the medical car, or other intervention cars, so that we would not be faced with this problem again.

There was much criticism, however, about the lack of help we received from the Spanish marshals. Rubens Barrichello, who is a good friend of Haberfeld, was upset that it had taken so long to get the boy out.

In the race itself, Mika Hakkinen was unassailable and David Coulthard came an excellent second. Rubens Barrichello took third place, with Ralf Schumacher, in the Williams BMW, fourth. Michael Schumacher came a lowly – for him – fifth, but took the two points.

It had been an exciting race and, of course, it was clear now that the struggle for the Drivers' World Championship was between Schumacher on thirty-six, Hakkinen on twenty-two, Coulthard on twenty and Barrichello on thirteen. In the constructors' race, Ferrari now had forty-nine points and McLaren forty-two. What would Nürburgring bring?

Sunday had been a pleasant day and Coulthard had raced brilliantly. He achieved a remarkable feat in getting a podium finish, despite his discomfort. At the end of the race, it took him time to extricate himself from the car as the continual pounding of the vibration of the car and pressure from his safety harness had accentuated his pain. I arranged with him that he would see me in London the next week, and that we would screen him completely to make sure that there was no other damage.

On the Tuesday afterwards he turned up at the Princess Grace Hospital where I practice in London. We scanned his spine with MRI, the magnetic resonance imaging system that shows the body with remarkable clarity. It confirmed that he had not hurt his spine, and that the site of the pain close to the midline at the back was where he had fractured three ribs. It took some time for the pain of the fractured ribs to diminish – as I found myself later in the year – about six weeks altogether. Four weeks later, I sustained my own injury in Monaco, so for a month or so after that Coulthard and I exchanged progress reports on our ribs.

EUROPEAN GRAND PRIX

In my experience the old circuit at Nürburgring was the most terrifying of all time. Situated in mountainous country, Nürburgring is subject to vagaries of weather, like Spa. I went only once to the old circuit when there was a race – in 1962, when it rained all weekend and Graham Hill won, with John Surtees second, Dan Gurney third, Jim Clark fourth, Bruce McLaren fifth and Ricardo Rodriguez sixth. What a line-up of talent! The circuit was very long, fourteen miles, and the lap time eight or nine minutes – there were only fifteen laps but that added up to over 210 miles. In that particular race, records reveal that Clark passed seventeen other competitors in one lap in the rain! I have a later memory of seeing Jackie Stewart on TV, in the 1968 race, dropping his car into the Karussel at a frightening pace when he won the race in masterly fashion, and Graham Hill, who was second, was four minutes behind! The race was run in foul conditions – torrential rain and fog. Big balls were needed to race there. In good weather the scenery is beautiful and the old circuit through the forest picturesque. If the weather's bad, you can't see it! I have driven it only once in a road car, in dry conditions, and the undulating bends, many of which are unsighted, are daunting and, of course, unprotected.

Above: Brazil, 2000. Eddie Irvine ruefully examines his wreck. After a crash in Japan 1999 he checked his watch when we arrived and said 'Where have you guys been?'

Right: Australia, 2000. 'Mr Cool Guy' said to Frank Gardner – when rescued after a high-speed shunt – 'Please turn off the air-conditioning as it upsets my nose.'

Above: Austria, 2000. The medical car team cheerful at Karl-Heinz' post-race party – Gary Hartstein and Jean-Jacques Isserman, longstanding, indispensable friends.

Below: Nurburgring, Germany, 1998. Herman 'the German' – excellent, forceful FIA medical car driver and his gift – daily cigars.

Above: Monaco, 2000. Traffic jam. Leow's bend after the second start, our medical car blocked against the Armco.

Below: Austria, 2000. First corner, accident – Schumacher's and Fisichella's cars – Giancarlo hastily departs the scene of the crime.

Above: Austria, 2000. 'Lucky Chaps' who escaped the first corner schemozzle: Hakkinen and Coulthard not involved, Barrichello recovered.

Below: Indianapolis, 2000. Awesome circuit, massive stands. The long straight is very fast in the FIA medical car.

Above: Johnny and Eddie: irrepressible, fun chaps, trendy shades!

Right: Jenson Button: steady eye, unusual talent, wonderful start.

Below: Germany, 2000. Over-enthusiastic Fisichella rams Schumacher's rear.

Above: Nurburgring, Germany, 1999. Pedro Diniz in the Sauber-Petronas gets a launch in the first corner accident.

Below: The car bounces and turns upside down losing the rear roll safety protection hoop in the process.

Above: Pedro Diniz was unhurt. While upside down he gave us 'thumbs up' to indicate he was OK.

Below: Karl-Heinz Zimmerman (on my left): Wonderful host, wonderful sense of humour. Eddie Baker (TV guru) holds the cake, Charlie Whiting (Race Director).

Above: Malaysia, 2000. First corner accident, Diniz crashes into Heidfeld; de la Rosa was also side-lined. Salo, Alesi and Zonta escape as do Mazzacane and Gene.

Right: Grand Prix Drivers' Golf Day, Murhof, 2000. Support from F1 drivers and teams over the years for the Brain and Spine Foundation was and is wonderful.

Despite this, in 1975 Niki Lauda lapped the circuit in less than seven minutes to go on pole – the only driver ever to do so. Later he said that to achieve this he had gone flat out through the final kink, and that that day he was 'in a special state of mind'. After his 1976 accident, the circuit was not used for Grand Prix racing again until 1985. By then, the new one had been built and the German Grand Prix was held there that year rather than at Hockenheim. Since 1997 the Grand Prix of Luxembourg, or Europe, has run there, usually in September. In 2000, though, the race was to be in May and we were hopeful of good weather in view of this.

The circuit facilities are very good at the new Nürburgring, and the hotel is near enough to walk under the circuit to the paddock. The medical headquarters are extensive and the equipment first rate. The Chief Medical Officer there is Dr Klaus Zerbian, a surgeon, who has worked with the Oberest Nationale Sportkomission (ONS) as one of the Porsche rescue doctors for many years. He and I have worked together often at the sharp end in Hockenheim, and I have the greatest confidence in him. The ONS rescue crews are always at Nürburgring, as indeed they are at Hockenheim, and in great strength. Usually there are three rescue helicopters with professional crews; the receiving hospital at Koblenz University is easily reached by air. The road approach to the circuit is somewhat tortuous and the traffic during race weekend very heavy so it really is a mercy to stay on the spot.

The weather lived up to our worst expectations, and on Saturday rainstorms were the order of the day. At the beginning of qualifying practice, the circuit was still damp and the track was declared wet. Usually in these circumstances there is a rush to get an early quick lap in case the weather worsens

– a so-called banker – and Rubens Barrichello set about this early on. Shortly after, Mika Hakkinen came out and did a time to put him on provisional pole. In short order, thereafter, David Coulthard appeared and went quicker, but almost immediately Michael Schumacher had a quick one, and was half a second faster. Later Coulthard took pole back, so the order was Coulthard, Schumacher, Hakkinen, Barrichello, when it started to rain heavily and practice ceased for a while.

After ten minutes, the rain stopped and out came the cars to try to improve their times. The first four remained unchanged, with Ralf Schumacher fifth and Jarno Trulli sixth. Jenson Button got himself up to eleventh and Pedro de la Rosa twelfth. Fingers crossed for Sunday.

Fortunately, at the start of the race the circuit was dry, though the overcast skies threatened rain. We waited at the entry to the pit lane alongside the ONS Mercedes rescue car driven by Jürgen Ditzinger. As the Formula One cars went by, we moved into position and went round the last curve to enter the pit straight. The start was clean, for everyone except Trulli, who was knocked off at the first corner – but no worry for us – and we took up our place behind the Armco just beyond the pit exit where we have easy access to the medical centre. We had a TV set alongside the medical car so we could see what was going on. Hakkinen had made one of his masterly starts and, from the second row of the grid, he took the lead, followed by Michael Schumacher. Coulthard and Barrichello followed, and Jacques Villeneuve had shot up to fifth from ninth on the grid. Once it started to rain, Schumacher closed on Hakkinen and performed one of his favourite manoeuvres which he uses at Nürburgring, driving up the inside of the Veedol chicane and emerging in front. By now it was raining heavily and Barrichello got past Coulthard. Of course, as usual the need for a pit stop to change to wet tyres produced anomalies and de la Rosa, who was going well, found himself in fourth spot behind Schumacher in the lead, Coulthard second and Hakkinen third. Barrichello had fallen back to eighth after his pit stop for wet tyres.

Conditions worsened but Hakkinen caught Coulthard and passed him, while Barrichello worked his way up to fifth behind Giancarlo Fisichella. During the mid-race pit stops Hakkinen took the lead by staying out, but lost it to Schumacher when he had to pit. Thereafter, Schumacher had everything under control, although Hakkinen closed the gap. One lap down, Coulthard took third and Barrichello fourth, Fisichella was fifth and de la Rosa stayed in the top six. As a result of the pit stops and the changes in the weather, one of the Minardis driven by Mazzacane came in eighth! Button was tenth. Schumacher was now on forty-six and had an eighteen-point lead on Hakkinen who had twenty-eight. Coulthard was four points behind on twenty-four and Barrichello, was not in contention. In the constructors' battle Ferrari had sixty-two points and McLaren fifty-two. Six races down and eleven to go, it was still early days – but perhaps in Monaco we'd get some decent weather.

MONACO GRAND PRIX

I suppose the best fun of the Monaco weekend was the medical car crashing during the safety exercise on Saturday morning. The normal procedure on Saturday morning is for the medical car to follow three laps at top speed around the circuit in pursuit of the safety car, which runs ahead, as it would in front of the Formula One pack if it had been deployed to control a difficult situation on the course. The first lap is designed to test the correct display of so-called SC (safety car) boards, which indicate that the safety car is on the circuit, and to ensure that the yellow flags are being waved all around the circuit to add more weight to the information displayed. On the second lap, usually, the safety car is called in and the medical car behaves as if it was the leading Formula One car, and continues to take a third lap, during which we confirm that the SC boards and yellow flags have been withdrawn, that the green light is on at the start–finish line on the course and that green flags are displayed all around it to inform the drivers that the race has been restarted.

Over the preceding year we had had some trouble with the electronic stability programme (ESP) on the medical car. This system is designed to help the average driver control a car; sensors detect any wheel slippage, and, if there is, the engine revs are cut down automatically by a computer to regain control. There is also a system to prevent the wheels locking under braking – ABS or anti-lock braking system. All racing drivers hate ESP vehemently. The first time that Frank Gardner drove the Mercedes in Melbourne with the system we were unable to turn it off. When it came into action Frank groaned and said, 'This car was designed for my granny to drive.' Subsequently we had it modified so that the system could be switched off, and this is the normal operational manoeuvre we perform whenever we're doing quick laps. However, on several occasions the previous year, when running on kerbs of a particular corrugation, the frequency of the vibration of the wheels had been switching the system back on, which was most disconcerting.

At Monaco, as you exit the tunnel the course descends to the harbour and a chicane which links to the track that adjoins the harbourside. On the inside of the chicane there is a long corrugated kerb and an escape route for any car that is not going to make it through safely. As we hurtled through the chicane, on the second lap, the right-hand wheels of the Mercedes ran over the kerb and, sure enough, switched on the system. We were getting close to the Tabac corner at which time Alex Ribeiro, who was driving, had to brake heavily. For some reason the ABS system failed, all four wheels locked, we went into a long slide and the right-hand front of the Mercedes hit the barrier with an almighty thud.

When I saw that the crash was inevitable, I watched, with some interest, how the front of the car folded upon impact. I could see the pressure wave running through the bonnet from the front as it buckled progressively, came up and caught the windscreen. Alex was wearing a four-point harness and was well restrained in his proper racing driver's seat. Dr Robert Scarlot the Chief Medical Officer and the local French anaesthetist were in the back and unhurt. However, I was thrown violently to the left and forward, and as I was wearing only the ordinary passenger lap-and-shoulder belt, my torso rotated and I was aware instantly of severe pain down the left side of my chest. It was, of course, a classic seat-belt injury and I realized I had probably cracked a couple of ribs, posteriorly, and injured the joints between the ribs and the cartilage, anteriorly.

After the impact Alex, of course, was angry with himself and banged the wheel a couple of times while I said a few rude words. The engine was still running so he managed to back the car off the barrier and we set off to return to the pits. With the severe buckling at the front, though, the wheels were obstructed, and there was a good deal of clunking and banging. Every fluid that occupied various parts of the vehicle had escaped its usual environs so oil, water and hydraulic fluid were leaking into the saloon, and we soon detected the unpleasant vapour of the air-conditioning coolant.

Of course, the noise of the crash had been heard by all and sundry in the pits, and there was a great turn-out of mechanics, team members and drivers, who cheered, clapped and laughed uproariously at the painful progress of the medical car to the pit exit and its usual station. The accident happened just a few minutes before the first practice on Saturday morning so we had to find another vehicle. We requisitioned an M4 that was lying around, put in all the medical equipment and sat back to see what would happen.

I was in pain, so at the half-hour interval between the two morning sessions, I went to where we keep all our gear and dosed myself up with some analgesics. Of course, we took a lot of teasing – Max Mosley pulled my leg and plenty of people took the mickey out of Alex in the most outrageous way.

Qualifying went off without any problems, and then we waited to start the Formula 3000 race. I found the fast laps just before and at the start pretty painful, so at the end of the event I took myself back to the hotel and dosed up again with analgesics and a fair libation of what Innes Ireland used to call 'the Scottish wine'. Whisky is an extremely good pain-killer, but when you have taken enough to be pain-free, you are also pretty carefree.

I had another couple of shots while I was waiting for Guy Edwards, an ex-Formula One driver, to come and pick me up as we had arranged to go out together for dinner that evening. When he appeared I told him of the accident. Again, of course, there was the mixture of amusement and sympathy. We went off in his car and met his wife, Daphne, at the appointed restaurant. Keke Rosberg, the great Finnish Formula One World Champion, was at an adjoining table and enjoyed all the fun of the Professor's discomfiture. I reminded him of when I had had to inject his ribs before an Austrian Grand Prix. He had had a shunt in practice, had damaged them, and before the warm-up on the Sunday morning I had had to fill his painful ribs with large quantities of Xylocaine to give him some relief for the race.

We had to do the same for Alex Wurz later in the year at Spa, and again in Monza. He had hurt himself in a water-sports accident and was in sufficient discomfort at Spa on Saturday for Gary Hartstein to put in an intercostal block,* which he repeated on race day. Poor Wurz still had a problem two weeks later in Monza, and Gary repeated the procedure in the medical centre there.

Race day at Monaco was pleasant and summery, and we lined up to take the start in the usual way with my car parked up a little side branch of the circuit at the hairpin bend. Round came the cars and off we went. Suddenly there were red flags everywhere. We went round the whole circuit but could not find the cause of the problem. We lined up for another start and, lo and behold, as we went through Casino

---

* Local anaesthetic is injected around the nerves which run with each of the ribs to block the pain from the movement of the fracture during breathing, or exertion.

Square, out came the red flags again. On this occasion, however, we soon discovered the reason. Going down the hill towards the Leows bends we came across a traffic jam of Formula One cars. I do not know who had started it but there had been a coming-together of about six cars. Some were obstructing the circuit, and others were jammed into each other. The marshals were already trying to relieve the situation, and there was no way through for us, so we sat there until the circuit was cleared then went back to take the third start, which went off successfully.

In the race, Michael Schumacher had to retire with a broken suspension, but David Coulthard was in excellent form and won in fine style. Mika Hakkinen collected only one point in sixth place. Rubens Barrichello held the flag for Ferrari with second place, Giancarlo Fisichella was third and Eddie Irvine, to Jaguar's joy, fourth, with Mika Salo a commendable fifth.

Schumacher had spread the lead at Nürburgring to forty-six points against Hakkinen's twenty-eight and Coulthard's twenty-four – but now with the Monaco win Coulthard lay on thirty-four, twelve points behind the maestro. Hakkinen moved to only twenty-nine points and Barrichello was on twenty-two. The constructor points went, Ferrari sixty-eight, McLaren sixty-three – getting closer.

The problem with multiple starts and the inherent delays is that the race gets off up to an hour late. That matters little in the summer when the evenings are light except that it might mean missing the plane home. Herbie Blash and I were on a flight out of Nice, so we conspired to get away as soon as possible. We dashed to the hotel, changed, jumped into a cab and were in Nice on time. I also found time to take a fairly liberal quantity of the aforementioned painkiller, of the Red Label variety.

There was widespread publicity about the accident in the medical car, which was even reported in *The Times*. However, one of the more amusing accounts of the accident appeared in Jody Scheckter's column in *Autosport*, headlined, 'Never mind Sid you're still the best', and accompanied by a picture of the crumpled Mercedes. I am afraid the car had to be written off!

CANADIAN GRAND PRIX

Each time I go to the circuit on Isle Notre Dame, I think of the first time I went to Montreal in 1949 when I was a medical student. That summer I had planned to get a vacation job to earn some money on the side. I had a friend, a fellow medical student, Ron Miller, with a connection to the Canadian Pacific Steamships. He had done several trips on the SS *Empress of France* as the engineer's writer, and he asked if I would like to take over the job. I had never been to sea in a great liner before so I signed up right away. The ship sailed from Liverpool via Quebec City to Montreal and, I hoped, back.

The job was interesting and entailed compiling and co-ordinating the engine-room data – fuel consumption, fuel reserve, nautical miles sailed, slippage and engine performance – and presenting it to the chief engineer at noon each day and then to the bridge. I had a little office, a huge typewriter to type out the data and two fingers to do it with. I also had a little cabin, situated, it seemed, under the propeller shafts.

Each time the props came out of the water in heavy weather, they would run free and my cabin would vibrate so fiercely I had to hold on to the sides of my bunk.

Still, it was great fun, and I was befriended by two of the engineers, Jack Matthews and Arthur Bibby, with whom I shared large quantities of beer when they were off watch. In fact, we had such a good time that when I got back to Liverpool my mess bill was greater than my modest stipend and I had to borrow some cash to leave the job without owing the company money.

On the way to Montreal we had an added bonus that the ship was carrying a group of Canadians, 'Weston Girls' – young travellers whose educational trips aboard were funded by a Canadian millionaire called Garfield Weston, who had made his fortune in biscuits. As engineering personnel, the three of us were not supposed to socialize with passengers; only deck officers were considered sophisticated enough to mingle socially. But we were able to get near enough to hear the delicate, soft accent of the girls from British Columbia – with which in later life I came to be entranced.

When we arrived in Montreal, at the old docks, we went to explore what for me was another world – after ten years of war and rationing it was a revelation to see the vigour and life of the downtown city – bursting shops, the brightly lit streets, the scent of exotic perfume on the ladies, nylons for sale, the pungent smell of Gauloises and cigars, abundant fruit. I smuggled back to Britain a ham, a pineapple, cigarettes and nylons for my mother and sister. Exploration of the night-life took us to a smart club called the Gumbo where, once the management realized we were only window-shopping, we were escorted back to the door by a bunch of heavies who helped us physically down the steps to road level.

In the sixties, when I was working in New York, I revisited Montreal to savour the lifestyle of this wonderful city. I got to know the superb hospitals at McGill University, the Montreal Neurological Institute, the Montreal General and Notre Dame hospitals, and the neurosurgeons of those years, Claude Bertand, Jules Hardy and Gilles Bertrand. In earlier years I had met the great Wilder Penfield, master of the surgical treatment of epilepsy. Small wonder that I am comfortable now in the ambience of Montreal and accustomed to the excellent medical service at the circuit headed by Dr Jacques Bouchard and Dr Ronald Denis.

This was the eighth race of the season, which usually represents the half-way mark, but this year, there would be seventeen races as Malaysia had been added. The battle for the drivers' and the manufacturers' championships starts to become critical, and psychological factors came to the fore.

On Friday and Saturday the weather was good and the performance ran nearly normally with the usual four up at the front, two Ferraris and two McLarens. However, qualifying changed the order of things and Michael Schumacher took pole for the third time this year. After a big contest David Coulthard shared the front row, with his and Schumacher's partners on the second row, Rubens Barrichello being slightly quicker than Mika Hakkinen. Heinz-Harald Frentzen did a good job to get fifth, and Jacques Villeneuve courageously took the sixth spot with Ricardo Zonta not far behind in eighth.

From our point of view the weekend had been quiet, and

the only problem looming for race day was the weather. On Sunday morning the warm-up saw the two Ferraris go quickest, followed by the McLarens, with Pedro de la Rosa a respectable sixth. Then rain threatened.

We wait for the start well before the notorious right-angled kink at the pit entrance where the tarmac turns sharp right then sharp left with the added pleasure on the outside of unforgiving concrete. This turn has caught out many people over the years, including Jacques Villeneuve, Michael Schumacher and Derek Warwick, who had an epic shunt there some years ago. Where we wait, the Formula One cars are really going fast as it is at the end of the longest straight on the circuit, and even on the parade lap they look quick.

We lined up behind, took off and had a quiet lap. At the pit exit we noted that Schumacher led, followed by Coulthard, Villeneuve amazingly third, followed by Barrichello, Hakkinen fifth and de la Rosa sixth. Unfortunately, Coulthard stalled on the grid and his mechanics failed to get him off before a penalty was incurred, which dropped him to tenth.

Having secured third Villeneuve hung on to it for as long as he could, holding up Barrichello until drizzle made conditions bad and Rubens got past. It was generally conceded that Schumacher drove a great race, leading all the way except for a brief period after his first pit stop. Later Barrichello almost caught him but the rain forced everyone in for wet tyres and he lost a lot of time in the pits. In the end it was a Ferrari one–two with Hakkinen fourth and Coulthard out of the points. Villeneuve, who had driven so well, had one of his accidents at the hairpin while making a heroic attempt to take Ralf Schumacher but instead taking off both Ralf and himself. Not one of his better accidents!

At the end Schumacher had opened the gap with fifty-six points against Hakkinen's thirty-two, with Coulthard on thirty-four and Barrichello on twenty-eight. Schumacher took his fifth win and was beginning to look confident. In the Constructors' Championship, Ferrari had eighty-four and McLaren sixty-six.

FRENCH GRAND PRIX

It is alleged that Jean-Marie Balestre had pronounced that Silverstone was at the end of a goat track! Some think Magny Cours would fit that description better. The circuit is in the bush and years ago was difficult to reach – although the road system has now been markedly improved. The circuit facilities are splendid, with a large paddock, good parking and excellent pits, pit lane and entertainment suites. The medical centre is one of the best in the world and the medical staff, under Dr Alain Chantegret and his deputy, well organized and trained.

Magny Cours is a pleasant little village, and lies close to some of the great wine centres of France – Sancerre and Pouilly Fumé. The countryside is pretty, so there are compensations for the lack of a decent airport, the closest being at Clermont-Ferrand. In recent years I have stayed at the Holiday Inn at the circuit, so I could walk to the paddock. The hotel is pleasant and well run, but remarkably expensive – last year I was presented with a bill for 67,000 francs for a room for four nights for my daughter (roughly £6,700). As Alex Ribeiro said, you could buy a small car for that amount of money.

One of the rituals on Thursday night at Magny Cours is for Jean-Jacques Isserman, Dr Chantegret and me to dine at a splendid restaurant with a splendid reputation – the Renaissance – where many VIPs eat. When I got the bill I realized you could bleed yourself dry there in a week. Nevertheless, you get used to the way in which the hoteliers' and restaurateurs' greed inflates the prices when a Grand Prix is in town. In one place in the UK recently dinner was £100 per person, without wine, and the rooms £600 per night with a five-night minimum stay.

Overall, I suppose, I preferred going to the French Grand Prix in the old days when it was held at Paul Ricard, where the atmosphere was more festive and the coastline so attractive, with charming seaside villages and the old hotel at Le Castellet. It was rumoured at one time that the Grand Prix might go back there but rumour is so rife in the Formula One world that when Derek Ongaro, the first permanent Formula One starter, and I saw shirts with 'RUMOURS' inscribed on the epaulettes we bought several each.

In central France the weather in June is usually excellent and this year Friday was no exception. But storms build up there, and on Saturday afternoon and night there was heavy rain. Fortunately, qualifying was over before it started.

The qualifying session was interesting, with Michael Schumacher setting a fast lap early on, which stood fast and put him on pole. David Coulthard was in with a chance to take it from him but spun and had to settle for second. Rubens Barrichello and Mika Hakkinen took the second row followed by Ralf Schumacher, Eddie Irvine, and Jacques Villeneuve in seventh place.

Race day was hot and steamy, and in the warm-up the McLarens took the first two places, then Schumacher, who was separated from Rubens Barrichello by the intrusion of Jarno Trulli. Eddie Irvine held on to sixth place in that session, no doubt raising the hopes of Jaguar supporters.

Half an hour before the pit exit opens we always do an inspection lap of the whole circuit to make sure that all the ambulances, medical-intervention cars and medical personnel are on station, that the helicopters are ready and the consultant staff in the medical centre are on the *qui vive*. It was hot and sticky as we went round, and I remembered a similar inspection lap some years ago, before Saturday qualifying practice at Magny Cours, in similar conditions. On that occasion, it was about forty-five minutes before the session was due to start and, sure enough, everyone was where they should have been and in order. I went off for some coffee in the paddock.

Ten minutes later when I got back to my car at the pit exit, I was astonished to find a blockade of the pit lane by all the French doctors, nursing staff, ambulancemen and God knows who else. There was a lot of angry shouting and fist-waving and obviously no possibility of starting the qualifying until the dispute was settled. I asked what the problem was, and was told that the circuit organization had failed to deliver lunch and Evian water around the circuit due to some internal disagreement or inefficiency.

Then Jean-Marie Balestre appeared in a car and shouted to me, 'What is the problem?'

I shrugged my shoulders. 'It is a French problem.'

Jean-Jacques Isserman and Dr Chantegret sorted it out

and the revolutionaries retired to their assigned positions. Napoleon claimed that the French army marched on its stomach and I guess it's the same for the doctors.

This year there was no such fracas and we went round to our normal waiting place, beyond the last corner before the pit straight near the final chicane as you come downhill from Château d'Eau. We are unsighted here, only being able to see the people on the back row of the grid, so we need to be informed if anyone fails to leave or is late in leaving on the parade lap. I have a strong objection to being hit up the rear by an excited Formula One driver barrelling round the circuit thinking he's late for school. Herbie Blash and I have a ritual exchange as the parade lap moves off, and we do the same if a race car is expected to start from the pit-lane exit as a result of being late or stalling on the grid. In this case the rule is that the miscreant may leave the pit exit after the last race car has passed it. With the differential in speeds this is just when we arrive opposite the pit exit as we go flying down the pit straight. Here the pit exit soon puts you on the racing line so we have to be particularly careful to avoid being T-boned.

That nearly happened to me in 1987 in Austria, when, at the third attempt to start, six Formula One cars exited the pit lane as the ONS Porsches arrived, including mine, with Herbert Linge driving, and we had to perform evasive action.

This time, at Magny Cours, Herbie Blash announced that all the cars were away and that there were no stragglers. Round came the twenty-two cars, we jumped on the end and got away without trouble. Apparently, it was not so clean up at the front where David Coulthard felt that he was obstructed by Michael Schumacher pulling across him in what is now known as 'the Imola manoeuvre' – a repeat of this year's start dispute at Imola. Fortunately, there was no collision and Schumacher led with Rubens Barrichello second, the latter having got past Coulthard when he backed off to avoid a shunt. Coulthard was lying third and Mika Hakkinen fourth. Jacques Villeneuve had made one of his amazing starts, and went from seventh to fifth. Barrichello held up Coulthard for a while but was outbraked at the Adelaide hairpin, and yielded to Coulthard's courageous manoeuvre.

Between the pit stops, Coulthard caught Schumacher and got past him on the second attempt at overtaking him, despite a bit of tyre-banging. Hakkinen also caught Schumacher and passed him – so on form were the McLarens. When Schumacher's engine failed Barrichello came in third. Villeneuve drove a great race and took fourth, Ralf Schumacher fifth and Jarno Trulli sixth. Jenson Button, who had started tenth, also put in a great performance by capturing eighth and nearly seventh, but just couldn't get past Heinz-Harald Frentzen.

The gap in the drivers' title had closed again. Coulthard, with ten points, went to forty-four, and Schumacher, failing to finish, stayed on fifty-six. Hakkinen picked up six to reach thirty-eight, Barrichello four so that he now had thirty-two. McLaren's one–two finish meant that with eighty-two points they were now only six behind Ferrari in the constructors' struggle.

AUSTRIAN GRAND PRIX

After a gap of ten years we have been coming to Österreichring, now called the A1-ring, at Zeltweg, since 1997. At the last race on the old circuit in 1987 we needed three starts to get going; the first two were a massive shambles. The circuit is much changed, with the most fearsome and fastest sectors removed. It remains spectacularly beautiful, and the facilities are very good, with an excellent medical centre and staff under the overall management of Professor Wolf.

This year I went there early and arrived in Graz on the Tuesday before the race, to play golf – or to provide entertainment for the other players and spectators – at the annual Grand Prix Drivers' Golf Day held this year at Golf Club Murhof at Frohnleiten near Graz. Christof Ammann and Dr Georg Reutter had made this possible and were organizing the Austrian round of the Ladies' European Open Championship there. All I had to do was lean on sufficient Grand Prix drivers and Formula One personnel to turn up early on 12 July, the Wednesday before the Grand Prix, at this superb golf hotel resort.

The idea was that each team would be led by one of the professional ladies, such as Trish Johnson or Samantha Head, and the tournament would be played as a Texas scramble. This system is the best for me as it means that I can move my ball from wherever it lands (usually in water) to the best position played by a member of the team! Tennis star Tomas Muster and skiing stars, Franz Klammer and Egon Zimmerman, joined David Coulthard, Pedro de la Rosa, Jacques Lafitte, Paul Stewart, Ron Dennis, Mario Ilien (playing golf for the first time), Norbert Haug and Karl-Heinz Zimmerman as spectators. By clever manipulation on somebody's part, I played in Sam Head's team with Pedro de la Rosa and two other excellent golfers, one of whom had been the Austrian national champion, and we won. I made one contribution with a remarkably fortunate putt, and am now the proud possesser of a lovely decanter inscribed 'Winner of Ladies' Open Championship, Murhof, Austria 2000'! Having seen this piece on the sideboard in our dining room, some of my friends have wanted to peep into my wardrobe to see if I'm a cross-dresser! Everyone had a good time, and there was an excellent reception, auction and dinner. The epic event raised a welcome £40,000 for the research fund – much to the satisfaction of my old friend Jeffrey Rose, ex-chairman of the Royal Automobile Club, who is president of the British Brain and Spine Foundation, and who made an appreciative speech to all the participants.

The next day we moved to Zeltweg and readied ourselves for Friday practice. Here, my car sits in an Armco island between the pit lane and the pit straight. We can see very little there and that part of the circuit is uninteresting. The practices went uneventfully with Mika Hakkinen on pole and David Coulthard alongside. Remarkably, Rubens Barrichello outqualified Michael Schumacher, who was fourth; Ricardo Zonta outqualified Jacques Villeneuve, and got sixth place on the grid. A new face among the Grand Prix drivers was that of Luciano Burti who was called in to replace Eddie Irvine, who had had abdominal pain all day on Friday. The Austrian surgeons who saw him thought he might have appendicitis and advised him to go to hospital. After a discussion with me, he decided to head for the UK. I telephoned my old colleague Norman Williams, Professor of Surgery at the Royal London Hospital, to make the arrangements, and Irvine left on Friday evening. Fortunately, he did not need surgery. When it was generally known that Irvine was in hospital, it is alleged a former driver said, 'Maybe he had to go because he hadn't been laid for twenty-four hours.'

Race day dawned fine, and as we waited for the start we were told that Burti would be starting from the pit lane and might well be exiting it as we arrived from around the corner. In fact, it didn't matter because there was a big mêlée at the first corner. We could see the dust flying as we barrelled down the pit straight. Arriving at the corner we came across Zonta, who had knocked Schumacher sideways so that he was now facing the wrong way. Barrichello was in the gravel and Jarno Trulli, having qualified fourth, was in a tangle with Giancarlo Fisichella – both of them out of the race. The McLarens had gone. Barrichello recovered and left the scene. Schumacher had completed his spin, stalled, and was now blocking the circuit, and out of the race. Somehow or other, the remainder of the pack got through, as did we, and we finished the first lap.

Pedro de la Rosa, who had started twelfth on the grid, found himself fourth on the first lap and drove an excellent race, getting up to third place until lap thirty-one when his gear-box failed. Clearly the golf before the Grand Prix had been a tonic for the young Spaniard – he might become a fine golfer if he plays regularly. Barrichello took over and kept third place. Hakkinen and Coulthard kept the lead between them and ended first and second, respectively, considerably reducing the points gap between themselves and Schumacher. At the end, the latter was still in the lead on fifty-six, but Coulthard at fifty and Hakkinen at forty-eight looked menacing. Barrichello had thirty-six points. In the constructors' title McLaren now seemed to have overtaken Ferrari – ninety-eight points to ninety-two. However, owing to a technical infringement on McLaren's part, the ten points due to Hakkinen's win were rescinded, reducing their score to eighty-eight.

There was a happy ending, however, for Eddie Irvine. When I spoke to Professor Williams, he told me Eddie had recovered and left hospital – most of the nursing staff having fallen in love with him!

GERMAN GRAND PRIX

For the Hockenheim race we stay at the Holiday Inn in Waldorf, and everyone seems to know it for there are always crowds of fans hanging around the front entrance to catch a glimpse of their heroes and to beg an autograph. It is a struggle to get in, and even early in the morning the hardiest supporters are there. The hotel is on the edge of Waldorf, a pleasant village, and the drive to the circuit is short and uncluttered in the early morning. Our usual crew assembled there on Thursday evening – Gary Hartstein, Alex Ribeiro and myself. Alex had spent an hour that afternoon practising with the medical car. The weather had been excellent but that was the end of it, and for the rest of the weekend conditions were turbulent, providing plenty of excitement as well as annoyance.

The Chief Medical Officer at Hockenheim is Dr Klaus Zerbian, also the boss at Nürburgring and, of course, the ONS provides the circuit medical rescue and the consultant medical staff. The medical centre, recently built in a secure site, is well designed and well equipped, and the surrounding hospitals at Heidelberg, Mannheim and Ludwigshafen are all excellent.

Heidelberg is a university town, with many historic build-ings. The medieval part is charming with its pedestrian-only

71

streets and setting on the banks of the river Necker. Over-looking the town is the massive castle, which dominates the southern skyline. In the middle of the old town there is an excellent medieval hotel at the edge of the central square, Hotel Zum Ritter. It has a wonderfully ancient dining room and serves the best wild boar and venison.

It was dry for Friday's practice, and the usual four were up at the front, but Jenson Button had performed well and was seventh. After the afternoon session there was a torrential storm and the exit tunnel from the circuit flooded so badly that the fire brigade had to pump it out to get the traffic moving when we came to leave the paddock. We set off later than usual because the FIA medical team always covers the Formula 3000 practices and races, and both the circuit and the pit lane were so badly flooded that the two thirty-minute practice sessions had to be postponed. Ultimately only one session of forty-five minutes was run, starting at 6.45 p.m.

Saturday, too, was dogged with rain, but the morning practice ran smoothly, although Michael Schumacher crashed his race car at the Agip curve in the Motodrom. This was towards the end of practice but he was cheerful and smiling when we picked him up in the medical car.

At the start of qualifying in the afternoon the circuit was damp after a few showers between the sessions, but the sky looked threatening. In consequence, all the cars powered out on to the circuit to try to get in a good lap before the heavens opened. David Coulthard was the star and set a lap that nobody equalled. Then came the expected downpour. Coulthard had been one and a half seconds quicker than Schumacher, who shared the front row. Giancarlo Fisichella came next with Mika Hakkinen alongside, then Pedro de la

Rosa and Jarno Trulli on the third row. Jenson Button had a rough time and ended up sixteenth, but he was ahead of Rubens Barrichello, who had an even worse time with car failure. In the last few minutes he managed to get in a lap that put him eighteenth.

At the Sunday morning warm-up the circuit was patchy, dry and wet. Coulthard and Hakkinen were the quickest, then came de la Rosa and Schumacher, with Barrichello still way down at ninth.

At the start the circuit was dry. The ONS and the medical cars wait at the point where the long straight from the Ayrton Senna Kurve enters the Motodrom, which gives a fine view of the cars in single file as they go round the Sachs Kurve. We latch on to the back of them in the Agip Kurve. Everything went well at the start but there was evidence of mischief at the first corner. As we arrived we saw Schumacher in the gravel and Fisichella in the tyre barrier. Both men were obviously unhurt, so we carried on behind the pack. This was the second consecutive race Fisichella had taken out Schumacher and, once out of the cars, they continued their dispute. The cause of the accident had been Coulthard performing the Imola manoeuvre on Schumacher – vice versa for a change – which forced Schumacher into Fisichella's line as the young Italian, starting from third place, tried to get to the corner on the outside.

This was just the beginning of a race that was full of surprises. We had no more trouble on the first lap and took up our place between the pit straight and the circuit as it exits the Sachs Kurve, where there is a large TV screen.

Hakkinen had taken the lead while Coulthard was dealing with Schumacher, so the McLarens were first and second with

Trulli in third and de la Rosa in fourth. Barrichello was making great progress from eighteenth and after two laps was eighth and up to third by lap fifteen before his pit stop. Then we could not believe what we saw on the screen.

A lunatic was standing alongside the circuit on the long straight running through the forest. Then he decided to cross the circuit and proceeded to walk along the verge of the tarmac. I heard Herbie Blash on the radio asking the safety car to go out while the deranged one was caught. It had just come in again when Pedro Diniz shunted Jean Alesi at the Senna chicane. We saw Alesi spin wildly then hit the barrier in a big way.

Out came the safety car again, while the circuit was cleared of debris and the remains of Alesi's car. Alesi appeared unhurt and could be seen standing inside the Armco chatting to an official. At this stage, after the second pit stop, the order on the tarmac was Hakkinen, Trulli, Barrichello, de la Rosa, Heinz-Harald Frentzen with Coulthard in sixth.

Then it started to rain heavily in the Motodrom, less so out in the country. Most of the drivers came in for wet tyres but Barrichello, Coulthard and Frentzen stayed out and were in the first three positions, with Frentzen threatening Coulthard. The latter came in for wet tyres, and Frentzen's car failed. This left Barrichello in the lead, Hakkinen second and Coulthard third, and this was how they stayed, which meant that Barrichello won his first Grand Prix. Everyone was pleased for him as he's a great guy and had at last fulfilled the potential he showed so long ago at Donington in the wet in 1993 when Senna put on such an electric performance. It was his 124th Grand Prix but his first win – better late than never.

Jenson Button put up his greatest performance so far.

Having qualified sixteenth he stalled on the grid before the formation lap began, so he started the race at the back. Then he moved inexorably up the field and finished fourth. Mika Salo took fifth, de la Rosa an excellent sixth and Ralf Schumacher seventh, after a Zonta shunt up the rear precipitated a repair in the pit.

In the points score, Schumacher had none to add so stayed on fifty-six, Coulthard with four moved to fifty-four, Hakkinen with six went to fifty-four, while Barrichello, with ten, stood at forty-six. Only ten points separated the top four contenders – and Barrichello was now among them. With the McLarens getting ten points in the Constructors' Championship and Ferrari the same, the scoreline read: Ferrari 102, McLaren Mercedes 98. Everything was getting tighter in both categories.

HUNGARIAN GRAND PRIX

Budapest is one of the great cities of the world. The frontage along the Danube as one looks south across the river is spectacular, with the ancient architecture of the Fisherman's Tower, St Mathias' Church and the beautiful bridges spanning the river. Formula One first went there in August 1986 for the inaugural Grand Prix of Hungary. In those days, Hungary was still behind the Iron Curtain in the grip of the Soviet Union. Many of us drove from Vienna, and it was an experience getting through the border control, which was just like a movie set, with fortifications like a concentration camp and Communist distrust of our contingent. Fortunately, we had been given papers that afforded us special priority but without this privilege the scrutiny to which we were exposed would have been even more stringent.

Once into the country, the roads were poor and the driving poorer while the road cars were the dreariest-looking devices I had ever seen. The countryside was pretty on the way to the capital and many fields were filled with masses of enormous sunflowers, their faces all turned to the sun.

On arriving downtown I was struck by the beauty of the old city on both sides of the Danube: it was so out of character with the dreary Communist background. The Margaretha bridge, the Chain bridge and old hotels, such as the Gellert on the south side in Buda, provided a lovely backdrop to the river – which was by no means blue! Derek Ongaro, the FIA crew and I were staying on the north bank, in Pest, at the Duna Intercontinental Hotel – where we have stayed ever since, although it is now the Marriott. In the old days it was a dreary place with a rather dark foyer and reception area, and a gloomy bar. The darkly stained wood and décor in the bedrooms reinforced its oppressive air. So much so that I looked around the room for bugs – of the electronic type! The telephones did not work, and neither did the air-conditioning. English was not spoken, the service was abominable, slow and surly. Only the wonderful sunshine and the view across the river counteracted the atmosphere. In the restaurant in the evening, however, the food was good and Hungarian musicians appeared with violins and played music, whose mood alternated between exhilaration and melancholy.

The next day, driving to the circuit past the opera house, the Square of the Great Heroes, with its wonderfully fierce statues, the art museum and the spa bath-house, I sensed again the medieval splendour of the past. At the circuit I met

Dr George Nemes, a Hungarian orthopaedic surgeon who had trained at the Birmingham Accident Hospital, which I had visited to see Mike Hailwood after the terrible road accident in which he sustained his fatal injuries.

George Nemes was an excellent chap who spoke good English, and later we visited the Institute of Trauma, and the Burns Centre, the designated hospitals where George was to introduce me to the staff.

At the Burns Centre, when I was in the director's office, I noticed some army helmets that I recognized from the Vietnam War. I asked about their origin – 'Vietcong', I was told; Hungary had sent medical teams to North Vietnam to help the Vietcong in their war against the USA.

When we left George's car on a public road outside the hospital grounds I noticed he did not lock it. On returning to it, I remarked upon his confidence that he would not be robbed. He replied, with a grin, 'There's not a lot of crime when the salt mines are just down the road.' And, of course, he was right, for there were Soviet army officers everywhere, in distinctive large, round hats, and Communist emblems in abundance. When we had the official dinner at the Communist Party Headquarters, George was unusually quiet so I asked him why. He kicked me under the table and whispered, 'KGB.' That explained the peculiar atmosphere, with its air of threat and melancholy, about the city.

George had one more endearing characteristic – eccentricity – he enjoyed collecting memorabilia from graveyards, and had at his home an aggregation of bits and pieces of flowerpots, statues, gravestones and other interesting bric-à-brac he had acquired when he had ascertained that he would not be caught grave-robbing.

77

Now the city is Westernized. Its beauty is unchanged but it is happy and gay. Prices have risen in the hotels, restaurants and shops with the introduction of capitalism, while crime, prostitution, bars, pornography and dangerous driving have advanced to such a degree that they are evident even in the 'best parts of the city'. Mercedes, Ferraris, Jaguars, Audis, Porsches are to be seen everywhere – almost to the same density as in Monaco. The hotels, of course, have been refurbished, and the Marriott, apart from its dark ground floor, is now light and gracefully decorated, the service excellent and the grilled goose liver, the *'specialité de la pays'*, washed down with a bottle of Egri Bikaver, or Bull's Blood, is an experience to be savoured. Bull's Blood was the staple drink of Hungarian warriors who made sure that they were high on it when they went into battle against the Turks. You don't have to go to Hungary to get it, and you must remember that red wine is awfully good for the heart and blood vessels in preventing heart-attacks and strokes. Even cardiologists admit it – and I know some who take it!

But I digress and must return to the 2000 Hungarian Grand Prix and the contest for the driver's and constructor's championships. Clearly this was a vital weekend, and a hot, humid one to boot. Not infrequently Hungary is the hottest place we go, now that we no longer go to Argentina and Brazil in January at the height of their summer.

On Friday morning we went to the circuit early as we had to reintegrate Jean Alesi. After the shunt he had had in Germany, in which he appeared unhurt, he had come back to the paddock, changed and left in his helicopter. He had been seen by a trackside doctor at Hockenheim, but had not checked in at the medical centre or with any of the FIA medical team because he had thought he was all right. However, for the next few days he had a headache, felt nauseated, but did not vomit, and was unsteady. He had phoned my office and in the interim had taken medical advice but he wanted me to check him out to make sure that he was okay to race at the Hungaroring. I had arranged to see him at the Hotel *Karpinski* where he stays in Budapest. This I had done, and neurologically he was perfect – even for a Frenchman – but we had to see him officially at the circuit medical centre with the chief medical officer, Dr Laslo, and Jean-Jacques Isserman. This we did, and he was cleared to drive.

The Friday practice was dry and hot, and at the end of the day both the McLarens appeared quicker than Michael Schumacher. But on Saturday morning the boot was on the other foot and in qualifying practice Schumacher had the edge and put himself on pole. David Coulthard made good time to gain the other half of the front row. The Williams BMW performed well and Ralf Schumacher took fourth place alongside Hakkinen in third, while Jenson Button made eighth. Rubens Barrichello was on the third row with Heinz Harald Frentzen alongside.

Race day really was hot, and we made the usual arrangements for when the heat load is high with doctors, fluid and intravenous kits available in the parc fermé at the end of the race in case of dehydration problems. However, the team gurus prepare their charges well; the drivers have a good fluid load aboard and are able to drink during the race if they so wish. Thankfully we do not see them collapse these days, as Nelson Piquet had in Brazil, and Nigel Mansell here, there and everywhere.

The warm-up saw Coulthard fastest followed by Schumacher and Barrichello, with Hakkinen fifth behind Ralf Schumacher in fourth and Frentzen lying in sixth. The day grew hotter and by race time it was the hottest so far of the year.

We wait for the parade lap in an internal road that enters the track before the last corner that leads on to the pit straight. We watched the cars go past then joined behind the two Minardis. There was no trouble at the start and the first lap passed without excitement for us.

But up front the excitement had happened as Hakkinen, from third, had made an electrifying start to shoot up the inside of Schumacher and reached the first corner in the lead. On the first lap Schumacher was second and Coulthard third. During the rest of the race, positions did not change for the top three, and Hakkinen drove a flawless race to pick up ten points and take the lead in the world championship with sixty-four points to Schumacher's sixty-two. With four points Coulthard went to fifty-eight. Barrichello worked his way up to fourth and was sitting on forty-nine. Closer than ever grew the contest.

Ralf Schumacher finished a creditable fifth, and Frentzen came sixth. Jenson Button hung on for ninth place. Next to the top four drivers, Fisichella was fifth in the drivers' category but on only eighteen points.

In the Constructors' Championship, McLaren gained fourteen points to go to 112, and Ferrari collected nine to go to 111. The Williams BMW cars were running third in the constructors' race, but a long way behind with twenty-four points. It was certainly a two-horse race in 2000, and one of them was prancing!

BELGIUM GRAND PRIX

I went to Spa on the Wednesday evening before the race because we had a meeting at the circuit of the research group on Thursday at 11 a.m. In the morning, the weather was good; the sun was shining and it was warm – I could hardly believe that I was in Spa – and this continued all day Thursday, all day Friday and all day Saturday. It was quiet, too, from our point of view, and we were able to sit inside the Armco at the La Source hairpin at the top of the hill looking down towards Eau Rouge and the very fast kink and blind climbing part of the circuit opposite.

However, this all changed on Saturday night and I woke to find pouring rain and puddles in the hotel car park. When we got to the circuit, half of it was shrouded in mist and it was continuing to rain heavily. At one stage I thought we would have to postpone the warm-up because on parts of the circuit you could not see the next corner for cloud or mist. However, I had a chat with McLaren's meteorological expert, who assured me that by nine o'clock it would be clearing, and when the warm-up was due to start visibility would be okay. I received this news with some relief because, of course, although we had helicopters at the medical centre and two were available, in mist it is difficult or impossible for them to fly, and the circuit is a long way from the major trauma hospital in Liège that we would use if we had a problem. However, the helicopter pilots told me that they were confident they could fly out but if they did have to go so early that morning they would not be able to fly back to the circuit. As we had two helicopters this didn't seem to be too much of a problem, and once the atmosphere cleared, my worries about the 'copters receded.

The warm-up began on a wet circuit, although the rain had stopped, and miraculously there were few difficulties although after about twenty minutes Fisichella, exiting from the corner near the medical centre, which is a fast right-hander downhill, got his wheels on to the white lines that outline the normal road, had a spin and hit the barrier very hard. The recoil inverted his car, the red flags came out and we charged off. It is quite a long way round the circuit to that point and, of course, Spa is the longest circuit on which we run. The accident had occurred just beyond the medical centre; the nearest fast car was already there when we arrived. Fisichella was out of his vehicle and climbing into the ambulance. We went on to the medical centre to await him. He arrived a minute or two later, stepped out of the ambulance with a grin and proffered the information that he was okay. We took him inside where the Belgian medical team examined him fully. We thought it best that he stayed there for the rest of the warm-up.

We set off back to the pit lane and I stopped my car at the Benetton pit to tell Flavio Briattore, the Benetton boss, that his driver was okay but I thought it better that he didn't try again in the warm-up period. Flavio agreed to this and the practice resumed, ending without any further excitement.

An hour or so after the warm-up it began to rain in a heavy and unrelenting manner. It lasted about an hour but then it stopped and our hopes of a dry race increased. The problem with the circuit at Spa is that the start–finish line is only a couple of hundred metres from the hairpin at La Source and the beginning of the downhill segment of

the circuit towards Eau Rouge. Invariably there are accidents there even in the dry, and in the wet it is inevitable
that collisions will occur as the cars brake and slide around
the tight-angled corner. Of course, in the old days before the
introduction of the safety car, there was no question of
the cars making anything other than a normal start. In fact,
in 1990, I remember making three starts as a result of
multiple shunts on the first lap at La Source before we finally
got the race going.

There was a good deal of discussion in the paddock as to
whether there would be a safety-car start. This is always a
difficult decision because it means that the cars go off in line
ahead. The mad dash to compete for the first corner is lost
and much of the excitement of the start is destroyed. About
a quarter of an hour before the pit exit opened, I asked
Herbie Blash what sort of start we were going to make
because, although the rain had stopped, the circuit still looked
wet. He replied that no decision had yet been taken but that
he would let me know when it had. This is of importance to
us because when the safety car is used we do not follow the
pack of Formula One cars: they are running slowly, or
relatively so, and when such a start is necessary it is not known
how many laps will be taken behind the safety car. It means
also that the cars are strung out in a very long line which
theoretically diminishes the chance of an accident when the
cars are ultimately released as the safety car comes into the pit
lane.

On this occasion, right up to the last few minutes, we
didn't have a decision, so Alex took the car out of the position
at La Source and we shot round the circuit to get into our
normal waiting position at Spa, which is in the escape run-off

area at Bus-stop chicane just before the pit straight. To my surprise, the circuit had dried out considerably and the line taken by the Formula One cars, during their fifteen-minute circulation after the pit exit had opened, had dried as a result of the repeated laps made by the twenty-two cars. It looked to me as we finished the lap that it would be perfectly all right to start in the conventional way. However, the circuit had looked so wet earlier that it was finally decided, just a few minutes before the parade lap, that they would start behind the safety car.

We waited in our allotted spot and the parade lap took place. The cars came back and settled on the grid. The starting lights went on, the safety car went off with the pack dutifully behind it in their respective positions. We followed them to the top of La Source and, looking down Eau Rouge, saw that there were no problems so we turned into the inside of La Source and took up our normal resting-place. After one lap, the cars were released and Mika Hakkinen, who had set the fastest qualifying time, got away in front of Michael Schumacher, but the cars had started on wet tyres and it was soon clear that they needed to come in for a change of rubber. This duly happened and Hakkinen was leading the race comfortably when he came down the hill towards the medical centre, made the same mistake that Fisichella had in the morning and spun violently. He caught the car brilliantly and ended up facing in the correct direction and was able to continue. However, in the time he lost Schumacher raced by and the contest between the two began again. The right-hand side of the circuit up at the top of Eau Rouge and beyond it to the first chicane had remained wet. Gradually Hakkinen caught Schumacher and made to go past him on this section of the circuit, but Schumacher performed one of his famous blocking manoeuvres and Hakkinen had to drop back at a speed of roughly 320 kilometres per hour. He settled down behind Schumacher but inexorably got on to his gear-box and, arriving at the same point of the circuit a couple of laps later, found Ricardo Zonta proceeding peacefully down that section on his own. Schumacher went to take him on the left side and Hakkinen, seeing an opportunity and taking the risk of running into the wet area, dived down the right-hand side of Zonta's car. He came out with an advantage over Schumacher and took the lead again as the cars entered the chicane. He managed to stay ahead of Schumacher, having performed one of the most daunting and courageous overtaking manoeuvres that I have ever seen in all the time I have been in Formula One. As the race proceeded, the clouds broke, the sun came out and the race ended in nice climatic conditions, the Spa weather having entertained us once again with such adverse conditions as to make the race very exciting. Hakkinen's lead went to seventy-four points against Schumacher's sixty-eight, Coulthard on sixty-one and Barrichello staying at forty-nine. Ferrari now had 117 against McLaren's 125 for the Constructors' Championship.

At the research group meeting on the Thursday, we had discussed once again the problem of cars losing their wheels and, of course, it had been recognized that the integral strength of the tethers was insufficient. This had been reinforced earlier in the season by our demand for the ties to be given a greater breaking strength. It had already been agreed that for next year two tethers must be attached to each wheel. We continue to be concerned about the possibility of a car losing its wheels, which might pass over the barrier, injuring spectators or circuit workers. We also worry that a car might be launched to fly over the safety and debris fences and produce a major catastrophe. This had happened earlier in the year when Zonta had had an accident in practice at Silverstone, although no one had been hurt. It turned out that our concerns were almost prophetic: at the next race, Monza, a wheel from one of the Jordan cars became detached and killed a fire marshal. Much development work needs to be done before these problems can be solved.

ITALIAN GRAND PRIX

I always worry about Monza. The circuit evokes in me the losses of the past. Particularly in the early morning, as the rising sun dispels the mist along the Curva Grande and the Lesmos corners, I feel the ghosts of the past. I have the same sensation when I drive through Flanders.

This year, however, my discomfort was reinforced when I went round the circuit on Friday morning and saw the layout of the new chicanes. We had always had a problem at the start: getting through the first chicane without an accident and, indeed, on one or two occasions, a funnelling of cars trying to get through it had caused the race to be red-flagged and forced to restart. Now the kerbs at the first chicane were lower but tighter. The escape route came out at a point near the exit of the chicane where a car using it might be at right-angles to the cars exiting from the chicane proper – all the ingredients for a T-bone accident. With the high noses of the Formula One cars, we were concerned about penetration of the cockpit in an accident occurring in that fashion. The second chicane had also been changed at the end of the Curva Grande and before the entry to the first Lesmo corner. It had been made faster, the kerbs were lower, and it looked a good deal less dangerous than the new first chicane. I suppose it's sod's law that that is where the first massive accident occurred on the first lap of the race.

The weather was fantastic, not too hot, brilliant sunshine, blue skies, and the rest of the circuit looked fine, with the usual masses of *tifosi* hanging around the paddock and filling the banks and the forests through which this circuit runs. We got ready for the first practice and made our inspection of the facilities in the medical centre, the helicopter, the fast cars and ambulances situated around the circuit. I always make a point of being meticulous about the inspections, and particularly so in Monza where, in the past, we have had lots of difficulties when the medical staff disappear into the bushes or the latrines. Together with Professor Ravelli, the Chief Medical Officer, and Dr Claudio, his deputy, we made the round and all was well. That morning the safety exercise on the circuit, in which we followed Berndt Mayläder in the safety car, was exciting. The circuit is very fast, and we did four laps. I found it particularly uncomfortable going over the kerbs of the first and, to a lesser extent, the second chicane. Our speed down through Ascari and on to the Parabolica was high: Alex was getting about 240 k.p.h. out of the Mercedes on this straight; the Formula One cars get up to 340 k.p.h.

The morning practice went off without event and, having had coffee with the Constructions Estintori Automatica (CEA) firemen, we returned to the medical car. There was no problem in the afternoon session, and afterwards we returned to Rosa and her CEA colleagues, for the usual magnificent lunch that is always held in the old cobbled paddock where the Formula One garages used to be in the sixties and before.

Saturday morning and afternoon qualifying were enjoyable, although Fisichella lost it at Ascari and hit the tyre barrier. On Saturday night Karl-Heinz Zimmerman held one of his splendid dinner parties in the motor-home in the paddock. One of the guests was the progenitor of the Cuban cigar industry, Aléjandro Robaina, now in his eighties, who had built a world-famous cigar empire. He was accompanied by his nephew and by Niki Lauda's right-hand man, Andrea Molinari. After dinner, the nephew produced a bag of cigar leaf and proceeded to roll for us all individually a fresh Cuban cigar.

Sunday morning was brilliantly sunny and warm, and the paddock throbbed with interest and excitement in view of the close struggle between Michael Schumacher, Mika Hakkinen and David Coulthard for the world championship. Schumacher was on pole, but the McLaren Mercedes team seemed quietly confident.

Just before the parade lap, and about eight minutes after the pit exit had closed, we donned our helmets and drove round to our resting-place at the back of the grid where the banking of the old circuit comes into the pit straight. We shelter there with the Ferrari of the CEA and an ambulance, which is, in fact, an intensive-care unit.

When the Grand Prix cars came round, we latched on to the back as they finished their parade lap. The starting lights lit in their usual sequence, went out rapidly and off we all went. To my surprise, all but two Formula One cars got through the first chicane without any difficulty, but we saw Eddie Irvine and Mika Salo in the gravel to the left of the first chicane obviously unhurt. As we pressed on, I heard Herbie Blash calling for the safety car to stand by. At first we thought it was because of the two cars we had seen in the gravel, but when we rounded the Curva Grande, we saw a massive accident ahead of us. A huge cloud of dust was hanging over the gravel, and I could see a tangle of wrecked cars, and debris lying around on the circuit. Some of the drivers were already out of their cars, but one of the Arrows cars was upside down. I felt sure that somebody had been seriously injured. We ran across the gravel to the cars, and saw Coulthard and Rubens Barrichello. The latter was upset, but seemed otherwise OK. Coulthard was cool and unhurt. Trulli and Heinz-Harald Frentzen appeared, and both seemed fine. The marshals were tipping Pedro de la Rosa's Arrows car from its upturned position, and he appeared, slithering his way out of the cockpit, unhurt. Then a marshal ran to us and indicated that somebody had been badly hurt on the left side of the circuit behind the Armco fencing. Gary Hartstein and Dr Lazzerino, the Italian doctor from our medical car, ran off with him to see what had happened. I told Alex that we'd better back the car down the circuit to be in contact with the accident.

We backed the Mercedes down the circuit about fifty metres, making sure that the safety car and the remaining cars in the race were not going to meet us full-on, and parked it on the left side on the grass.

We found Gary and Dr Lazzerino working furiously on a fire marshal, who had clearly been badly injured. I radioed to Herbie Blash that we had a seriously injured patient. Herbie asked if we could manage with the safety car controlling the pack. I replied that we could, and we did, but the lap time at Monza for Formula One cars led by the safety car is a bit under two minutes, so every two minutes or less, the cars roared past, weaving sinuously along the circuit to keep their tyres hot and the tyre pressures high. The noise makes communication difficult I took off my crash helmet. I handed the equipment Gary needed over the Armco and, with Alex, we summoned a stretcher and an ambulance.

In the meantime, Gary had intubated the patient and put up an intravenous transfusion, so all was ready to transport the marshal to the medical centre. It had taken us about twenty minutes to get to this point and I suppose, by then, the Formula One cars had done ten laps. Gary went in the ambulance with the Italian doctor and the patient, while Alex and I drove back to our place at the pit exit.

As the ambulance turned into the medical centre, and as Alex and I were on our way to our place in case our services were needed again, I heard the safety car being called in.

Gary and our Italian assistant reappeared and we settled down hoping that we were not going to have any more trouble in the rest of the race. A serious accident like that has a sobering and melancholic effect on us.

The Ferraris put on a brave display, and Schumacher won, with Hakkinen second, but the celebration was tempered by the sad news that the marshal had died.

The gap between Schumacher and Hakkinen was now only two points, seventy-eight and eighty respectively; for the Constructors' Championship, Ferrari had 127, four points behind McLaren.

After we cleared up and changed I went to Karl-Heinz's motor-home and was sitting there when Ralf Schumacher came in and asked if I would find out the name and address of the widow of the marshal. Tragically, Paulo Ghislimberto had been married for only a year and his wife was expecting their first baby. Then Michael Schumacher appeared and said that Ralf and he wanted to make a donation to her. He knew this wouldn't bring back her husband but at least she would be financially secure. Later that week, Bernie Ecclestone started a fund for her with a donation of $40,000 and asked each of the eleven teams to provide $10,000.

There was much comment in the newspapers and in the racing journals about the wisdom of continuing the race under the safety car for such a long period of time. It is not usual for Formula One cars to run for a prolonged period behind the safety car, and I think that there were technical reasons for wanting the cars to do fewer laps under the safety car and for the race to be stopped.

Two weeks later at Indianapolis, Bernie said he thought that if the safety car needed to be out for more than three laps the race should be stopped.

AMERICAN GRAND PRIX

In 1967 I saw this awesome banked circuit for the first and only time until I returned for the 2000 race. Many changes have occurred in the interim and the new Grand Prix circuit had been put in on the infield. It seemed to be rather tight and tortuous, although the short back straight looked quick and the entrance to the banked circuit from the infield and the exit from the bank circuit to the infield still looked pretty awesome.

Of course, the American fans were excited by the idea that the Formula One cars were going round in the wrong direction, namely clockwise instead of anticlockwise, and that they were going to race whether it rained or not, unlike other forms of motor racing in the United States.

In 1967, I was visiting my old pal Jim Rae, a crack orthopaedic surgeon who had been my colleague in the Upstate Medical Center in Syracuse. Now he was chairman of the Department of Orthopaedics at the University of Indianapolis. I had flown out with a young neurologist called David Haas, who was also a motor-racing fan. In those days I did not belong to a medical team that would have got me to the Indy race, so the three of us had bought spectator tickets and we were all agog for it. Our seats were not very good, right down at the front in the middle of the long pit straight, where the cars would pass too quickly to see them properly. But we enjoyed the warm-up to the event, which featured Purdue State Band, the Golden Girls and all the razzmatazz of American showbusiness.

One of the exciting features of the race was the introduction of a turbine car, to be driven by Parnelli Jones, which was familiarly called the 'Whispering Jet'. It fulfilled all expections and was very fast. But after eighteen laps, rain fell, the race was stopped, and we were all dismissed. As it was Memorial Weekend, we clinicians had Monday off so David and I stayed another night with Jim and went back to see the rerun of the race the next day. The weather was fine and, in fact, the rain had done us a good turn because most of the other spectators had to leave town and were unable to take their seats on the Monday. So we could choose where to sit at the back of the best stand. We ensconced ourselves and the race started. Soon Parnelli Jones was winning like mad, but in the last few laps a component on his car failed, and A. J. Foyt went past to victory.

In 2000, the excitement was all about the Hakkinen–Schumacher race for the world championship. After the Ferrari victory in Monza a couple of weeks earlier, it was clear that if Michael Schumacher won and Mika Hakkinen came second, then Schumacher would be in the lead for the world championship by two points. I arrived at the Indy circuit on the Thursday morning and had a look round the marvellous facilities within this great bowl. The stands are massive. There is an absolutely first-class medical centre and a fine medical team under Dr Henry Bock, who has been consultant-in-charge of the Indy medical centre and its track medical service for many years. I had met him before when he had come to Monza in 1999 to see how the FIA medical services differed from those he provided at Indianapolis. Earlier in the year Jean-Jacques Isserman had been to Indianapolis – so we were all well acquainted. It was easy to work together. On the Thursday Jean-Jacques took charge of the spinal extrication teams and practised with them and with the Jaguar chassis and the Lear seat we had been using to train our spinal extrication teams. By the end of the day, he was well pleased with the expertise of the American teams.

During the afternoon, I had been asked to go to a presentation about a new extractable seat, which had been developed by Lear at my request. The problem with the old seat was that when we got a driver out of the cockpit in his seat, we had then to take him out of the seat before he could be placed on a deformable mattress, which meant one extra manoeuvre that we wanted to avoid. Sure enough, Lear had solved the technical problem. The new seat consisted of an outer shell to give the seating integral strength and an inner shell that could be taken apart. Once the driver was out of the car in his seat, its buttock portion could be removed without disturbing the patient, and also the lateral aspects of the seat torso, leaving a spinal splint that extended from the sacrum to the top of the head would remain to immobilize the spine. It was a brilliant solution to the problem.

Eddie Irvine was also at the presentation (Lear having sponsored, first, the Stewart Formula One team and, subsequently, Jaguar), and there was a good turn-out of the press. Alex Ribeiro was there, too, and I valued his positive opinion of the new seat as, of course, he had been an experienced racing driver, including Formula One.

On Friday morning the weather was pleasant, but there was speculation that it might rain. However, the two practice sessions went off without any problems and the drivers seemed pleased with the design of the circuit, particularly enjoying the banked section.

That afternoon, a group of them had agreed to go to the children's hospital downtown in Indianapolis to sign autographs. Michael Schumacher, Heinz-Harald Frentzen, Jarno Trulli, Giancarlo Fisichella and Jenson Button came along, with Francesco Longanesi, the director of external and press relations for the FIA, and me. The great hall of the hospital was built like the atrium of a Hyatt Hotel, with those internal lifts that look rather like limpets attached to the wall going up and down. The children were all lined up with their mums and dads and three drivers signed posters for them while Trulli and Button posed with an empty chair in the middle so that each child could be photographed with them. We all had a good time, and before we left to go back to the circuit I overheard Button questioning a lady as to where the best nightlife was in Indianapolis. Apparently he had been out the night before and had found it a rather quiet and respectable town.

When I asked him what he thought of the circuit, he said it was terrific: 'the long straightaway, and underbraking at the end of it, made it possible to get a good tow and to overtake just as you entered the chicane or even during it.' His confidence in the circuit was not misplaced: he qualified sixth, after two Ferraris, two McLarens and Trulli's Jordan.

The paddock at Indianapolis is enormous, and although there had been heavy demand for VIP passes, it never looked crowded. Because it was such a great inaugural occasion, many people I had not seen for some years turned up. Phil Hill was there, with his lovely sense of humour – he was a bit anxious because his son was driving in the supporting Porsche Super Cup race. I also saw Jack Brabham, who was carrying a large birthday card for the old cronies to sign for Frank Gardner in celebration of his seventieth birthday. I met up with Tim Parnell, the ex-Formula One race driver and then, to my surprise, I spotted Dan Gurney, who was with Norbert Haug.

I hadn't seen Dan since Clay Regazzoni's accident in 1980, and I teased him about the time at Spa in 1964 when he was leading the race on his last lap for the Brabham team, and ran out of petrol. He sat in the cockpit disconsolate, and Graham Hill went past him to take the lead. Hill then ran out of petrol, too. Then Bruce McLaren appeared at La Source seemingly to win the race but he also ran dry and was freewheeling downhill to the line agitating the car. Suddenly

Jimmy Clark came round La Source, passed McLaren and won the race! Dan told me that he knew he was short of gas so he dived into the Brabham pit to get a squirt. There was none available. The mechanics had packed it up to go home!

I also saw Tim Schenken, the Australian Formula One driver and race director for many years in Adelaide and recently at Melbourne. He told me several jokes, which I cannot repeat here, but clearly he had been under the tutelage of Frank Gardner.

Saturday morning was pretty gloomy and it looked like rain but we came to the qualifying practice with the circuit dry. It started to drizzle as the cars shot out of the pit exit with most people trying to get a banker. To my surprise Michael Schumacher stayed in the garage until the rain stopped and the circuit dried up. Then he came out and got himself pole position with his usual brilliance. Coulthard was second, Hakkinen third, Barrichello fourth. Trulli and Button shared the third row.

That morning we had done the safety exercise with the medical car. I had enjoyed going round the banked circuit so quickly, and understood why the drivers loved it. It was good practice for us to do that safety exercise because we were going to follow the first supporting Porsche Super Cup race on Saturday afternoon after the Formula One qualification. When the time came, we followed the Porsches' parade lap and the first racing lap, and were able to keep within striking distance in the remarkable Mercedes we have as the medical car. In fact, on Sunday morning, when we followed the second Porsche Super Cup supporting race, which took place after the Formula One warm-up, the circuit was still damp after rain that morning, so the Porsches were slower and we sat on the back markers all the way round for both the parade and the first racing lap. One of the remarkable features about this circuit was that the Porsches' qualifying time was 1 minute 37 seconds in the dry and the Formula One cars' qualifying time was 1 minute 14 seconds, which meant that the Porsches were only 23 seconds slower than Formula One.

The American audience relished the thought of seeing racing cars in the wet. They got their wish in the warm-up on Sunday because the circuit was wet, but this did not deter the Formula One boys and they put on a good show for the crowds which now packed the circuit. It rained again after the Porsche race and it seemed almost certain that the Formula One race would be wet. But, surprisingly, when we went round to get on the back of the Formula One grid, just before the start of the parade lap, the circuit seemed dry.

The race was exciting: there were no snarl-ups at the start or going through the first chicane as they came off the banking into the infield. David Coulthard had been sharing the front row with Michael Schumacher, but had managed to get ahead. Then it was announced that Coulthard had jumped the start and was given a stop–go penalty. However, Schumacher overtook him in a daring and tricky manoeuvre, underbraking at the end of the long straightaway, actually the tricky first chicane. This put Coulthard out of contention. Then there was more excitement because everyone, except Johnny Herbert, had gone out on wet tyres, and would need to change them. Schumacher stayed out while everyone else was in the pits and built up a handsome lead. He then came in, changed his tyres and was leading the race comfortably when Hakkinen began to erode his lead. He got to within about five seconds of Schumacher when the McLaren Mercedes' engine caught fire and ended his race.

Thereafter, it was a matter of Schumacher maintaining his lead, but he nearly lost the car completely towards the end of the race when he spun. However, he recovered and finished comfortably ahead of Barrichello, who had gradually got himself into second place, with Heinz-Harald Frentzen third. The latter had been engaged with Villeneuve in a terrific battle for his place. Villeneuve had attempted to get past him several times, but had to settle for fourth.

There were, of course, huge celebrations from all the Ferrari fans for the Ferrari victory. This now meant that Schumacher on eighty-eight points, with Hakkinen failing to finish and still on eighty, was eight points ahead. In the constructors' contest Ferrari were on 143 points, with McLaren ten behind on 133. The contest was still tight, with Japan and Malaysia to come.

Immediately after the race I saw Ross Brawn, the Ferrari designer, who told me he had nearly had a heart-attack when he saw Schumacher spin, adding a few unprintable expletives. Later, Norbert Haug told me that Mario Ilien had gone trout fishing in Montana instead of getting back to the factory to find out what had gone wrong with Hakkinen's engine to make sure it wouldn't happen again. Nevertheless, Jürgen Hubbert, the Mercedes boss, whom I saw with Karl-Heinz Zimmerman shortly after the race, took the problem philosophically with a shrug of his shoulders.

JAPANESE GRAND PRIX

When I arrived at Suzuka on the Thursday afternoon before this crucial race for the world championship, I was reminded of my first time there in 1987. It had been my second visit to Japan and I had been invited to the neurosurgical department of the University of Hamamatsu where one of my old protégés and pupils, Kenichi Uemura, had become professor of neurosurgery and chairman of the department. I had helped in Keni's training when I was on the staff of the Upstate Medical Center in Syracuse, and he is one of the most brilliant men I have ever met.

I had left London on the Sunday and arrived at Hamamatsu on Monday afternoon, whereupon I was immediately put to work. First I gave a lecture, and then spent some hours talking with the research fellows who were working in Uemura's department, then went to one of the hospitals to do a ward round. Later I was taken to a restaurant for dinner and was liberally supplied with whisky. I got to bed at about 2 a.m., after my hosts had told me they would pick me up at six thirty the next morning!

Sure enough, at six thirty, they were in the lobby and I received a message to 'shake a leg'. That day included more ward rounds and a visit to the Suzuki car factory in Hamamatsu so that I could see how the Japanese workforce were managed. It was an impressive display of discipline, friendliness and cleanliness, and the facilities for refreshment and recreation were splendid. There was another social event that night, and by the time I left Hamamatsu on Wednesday morning to go to Suzuka, I was exhausted.

I arrived there mid-afternoon and asked for the chief medical officer. I was told that he had not arrived yet as he was very busy in Tokyo. I asked when he would appear and was told about five o'clock, so took the opportunity to go and look at the nominated receiving hospital for the Grand Prix. To my horror and disappointment I discovered that it was not up to the job. When I returned to the circuit at five o'clock there was still no sign of the chief medical officer and I was told he would be there probably by six. At six o'clock he still had not showed, and I was told he would be coming at seven. I decided to get tough and indicated to the FIA race director, Roland Bruynseraede, and John Corsmit, the permanent travelling FIA official steward, that I was unhappy with the situation. The Japanese authorities said they would make sure the chief medical officer turned up and suggested I met him at nine o'clock. I said, 'Actually, I'm going to bed now and we'll have the meeting at midnight.' Everyone looked upset about that, but I was determined, and went to bed for a few hours.

When I appeared for the meeting, everyone was assembled, including a rather lean Japanese gentleman, who I was told was the Chief Medical Officer. I opened the meeting by saying that I understood pride was an essential characteristic of the Japanese people, and if anyone had cause to be ashamed of himself then he might be invited to commit hara-kiri. This set the tone of the meeting, and apologies began to pour forth. Then I said that I was unhappy with the selected hospital and that alternative arrangements must be set up during the night with the University Hospital and the Serei Hospital, both at Hamamatsu, and with the nearby Nagoya Hospital. I pointed out that I would have to inspect these hospitals as soon as the arrangements had been made, and asked for a helicoptor to be made ready for the next morning.

This caused a flurry of excitement. In those days, when we were appearing at a new circuit, and before the first practice of the Formula One cars on Friday, it was normal for part of Thursday afternoon to be devoted to familiarization with the circuit and this was due to start at one o'clock. I said that everything must be in place by eleven o'clock on Thursday morning and retired to bed.

Next morning, I reported to the medical centre to find the helicopter waiting and that the arrangements had been made with the hospitals I had nominated. I took off in the 'copter, flew to Hamamatsu and to Nagoya, completed the inspections, and returned to Suzuka before eleven o'clock. The familiarization session started on time.

The next year when I returned, I found no evidence of the offending Chief Medical Officer and I have not set eyes on him since. Dr Kito, who had been an army doctor during the Second World War, had taken over. He was a strict disciplinarian and had everything in good order. When he retired, his son replaced him and is still the Chief Medical Officer.

On Friday morning at about ten o'clock we normally start to inspect the circuit and this year we did as usual with Jean-Jacques Isserman, Dr Kito and an interpreter. I was struck by the way in which the doctors had taken to heart the instructions I had given them in previous years. In every fast intervention car and among pit-lane medical crews, the doctors wear short white jackets with several pockets and 'Doctor' inscribed across the front. In their pockets, as I had taught them, they carry a laryngoscope, a tongue forceps, an endotracheal tube, Guidel airway and a stethoscope –

101

although I have never had much use for a stethoscope on the circuit. I had also taught them to take some adhesive tape off a roll and stick it to their jackets so that if they needed to put up an intravenous infusion, or insert an endotracheal tube into a patient, they always have the tape ready and do not have to struggle to pull it off the roll in front of a television audience. Sure enough, each chap had his two strips of zinc oxide tape attached to his jacket, ready for use.

Alex Ribeiro had been unable to come to this race because after Indianapolis he had had to go to Australia to the Olympics to fulfil his role as counsellor and pastor to the Brazilian athletes. In his place to drive the medical car was a gentleman with whom I had driven once before some three years earlier. Hideo Fukuyama told me proudly that he had won in his class in the Le Mans twenty-four-hour race some five years earlier in a Nissan car. I had already seen Herbie Blash, who told me that Fukuyama had done the normal one-hour practice on Thursday afternoon to verify that the driver knows the circuit well and that he can function at the appropriate speeds. Herbie and Charlie Whiting told me that Mr Fukuyama had performed exceptionally well, so I had no qualms about our driver. On Saturday morning we did the three-lap safety exercise with the safety car and all went perfectly, so we settled down to watch the practice and to get ready for what would be a vital qualifying session on Saturday afternoon.

We watched the qualifying on television as, at the point where the medical car sits at the exit of the road from the medical centre on to the circuit. The Japanese had thoughtfully provided a big screen, which is built into a cabinet so that the images are visible, regardless of strong sunshine.

At the qualifying session, Michael Schumacher dominated the proceedings as he had the practices. Mika Hakkinen put up a tremendous performance but we ended the session with Schumacher on pole, Hakkinen alongside him, David Coulthard third, Rubens Barrichello fourth and Jenson Button fifth. Button had again put up a terrific show, and it was clear that, with the consistent good form he was now displaying, he would be a force to be reckoned with in the future.

We had had good weather for Friday and Saturday but on Sunday morning rain was forecast and it was gloomy and dark with heavy cloud. The warm-up went off uneventfully and we settled down to wait for the start of this most important race.

It was scheduled for two thirty, an unusual time, but presumably Bernie Ecclestone determined this so that it worked internationally from the television point of view. Sure enough, at two o'clock the pit exit opened and the Formula One cars circulated for fifteen minutes until everyone had taken their place on the grid. At this point we donned our helmets and left the pit exit for our place at the back. The weather was now looking very threatening but by some miracle the rain held off. We waited while the cars did their parade lap and then hooked on at the back and went down through the chicane to take the start – I thought there would be a schemozzle at the beginning of the race, for Hakkinen and Schumacher would be hell for leather to get to the first corner in the lead.

The start went off brilliantly, without anyone left on the grid, and as we approached the first corner, I could see that they had all gone through and the pack was intact. There were no accidents of any significance on that first lap, so we took up our position at the exit from the medical centre and watched the screen. Hakkinen had made a miraculous start, although later I was told that Schumacher attempted to cut him off, and he was ahead. He held the lead then for most of the race, but at about the two-thirds stage it started to rain gently and it was clear that Schumacher was gaining ground. Sure enough, when Hakkinen came in for his second pit stop, Schumacher stayed out and, despite the slippery conditions and the fact that he was on dry tyres, he built up a considerable lead so that when he came in for his second pit stop, he was quick enough in the pits to come out still ahead of Hakkinen. As Hakkinen came down the pit straight, Schumacher left the pit exit in the lead. Thereafter, inexorably, he gained a greater and greater lead, took the chequered flag and the championship. Schumacher was now leading with ninety-eight points, with Hakkinen second in the fight on eighty-six, and in the Constructors' Championship, Ferrari had 156 points to McLaren's 143.

Of course, there were scenes of indescribable joy from the Ferrari team and everyone was kissing and hugging each other. Hakkinen got out of his car and congratulated Schumacher and the Ferrari team on winning the World Drivers' Championship as well as the race.

I spent the evening quietly and next morning was paying my hotel bill in the foyer when I saw Stefano Domenicali, the Ferrari team boss. I congratulated him and he reported that Schumacher had had an uproarious party and had outdone himself with the celebration. I remembered when he had won his second world championship at Aida, the other Japanese circuit where we had been in 1995. Schumacher was still driving for Benetton, and had been dancing on a table when I left the party. He and his team-mate Johnny Herbert had been soaked in champagne. I gather that similar frivolities had occurred this time but his companion had been Rubens Barrichello, who had come fourth in the race.

Stefano was glad that this particular battle was over and that the Malaysian event at Kuala Lumpur would be a more relaxed affair, even though the Constructors' Championship was still undecided and depended on the result of that race.

McLaren, of course, were disappointed not to win the Drivers' Championship but still had a chance with the Constructors' Championship, and Ron Dennis, being the courageous optimist that he is, would no doubt have been getting everyone into line to try to take that title in 2000.

MALAYSIAN GRAND PRIX

I had been downtown in Kuala Lumpur in 1999 to inspect the University Hospital, selected for us by the chief medical officer at the circuit, Dr Zin, who is a lieutenant colonel in the Malaysian army. I thought the hospital remarkable for the amount of work it got through. When I was walking through the out-patient department I was hailed from behind: 'Professor Watkins!' I turned to see my old senior house officer from the London Hospital, Dr Patrick Tan, who was now a consultant in Kuala Lumpur.

In 2000 I arrived in Kuala Lumpur on Wednesday so that I could attend a meeting of the Technical Working Group on Thursday morning. We had been allotted rooms at the Mandarin Oriental Hotel, slap in the centre of the wealthy district of Kuala Lumpur, which had been built in the wake of the discovery of oil and petrol in the country. As I looked out from the hotel's swimming-pool, on the third floor but hundreds of feet above the street, the spectacle was stunning: the pool appeared to flow right over the side of the skyscraper into the streets below. I could see, directly in front of me, a large park and in the distance the high-rise buildings of the Shangri-La Hotel and the Kuala Lumpur Tower, with its revolving restaurant. In the central area of the park there is an old colonial house, somewhat dilapidated, and a beautiful mosque. Behind the hotel are the twin Petronas Towers, named after the national petroleum company that had been responsible for the rebirth of Kuala Lumpur.

The year before, we had all been immensely impressed with the beauty and the quality of the facilities at the circuit, and the efficiency of the organizers. It lies a long way out of town, close to the new international airport, and on approaching it, I could hardly believe I was going to a racing circuit. The quality of the landscaping and the architecture of the stands and buildings is quite out of the ordinary. The garages and pit facilities are large and beautifully arranged with rooms immediately behind the work areas for the teams to take refreshment. Separated from this area by a walkway is a series of separate buildings, again beautifully designed and air-conditioned, for use as offices by the teams. The medical headquarters is a most functional building, and when we inspected it, we found that everything was in place, thanks to the efforts of Lieutenant Colonel Zin. Of the intensive-care unit, Gary Hartstein remarked that it was fitted with the best equipment we had seen all year.

The genius behind all this was a gentleman called Tan Sri Haji Basirbin Ismail, who is Chairman of the Sepang International Circuit Board. He is a generous and genial host, and he invited us all to dinner on Saturday night in the revolving restaurant at the top of the Kuala Lumpur Tower. The view from the top of this remarkable building is breathtaking, with floodlighting of the principal buildings at the central core of Kuala Lumpur, and the mosques.

The atmosphere at the circuit on Friday morning was much more relaxed than it had been at Suzuka now that the Drivers' Championship had been decided, but there was still the possibility that McLaren could win the Constructors' Championship. It seemed an outside possibility, for to wrest the championship from Ferrari McLaren cars would have to win the race and come second, and the Ferraris would have to gain no more than three points.

The practice sessions were conducted amid great heat, with the ambient temperature over 30°C and the track-surface temperature in the high thirties. The sessions were dominated once again by Michael Schumacher, and the contest for the quickest times was fought out between him, David Coulthard and Mika Hakkinen. Eventually, by Saturday afternoon, the grid was decided, with Schumacher on pole and Hakkinen alongside him. David Coulthard was third with Barrichello fourth, and the surprise of the weekend was the performance of Alex Wurz who, in the Benetton car, had been fast in the earlier sessions and qualified in fifth position with Jacques Villeneuve sixth.

Race day began in overcast conditions and from time to time it looked as if it might rain. The warm-up in the morning went without incident, and we made ready for the last race of the season. Just before the start, we did a lap of the circuit to get to the rear of the grid, and then with the start of the parade lap, we waited for the cars to come round. All twenty-two got away from the starting line, and as they passed us, we clipped on at the back and went to take the start. It is quite a short run down the pit straight from the start–finish line to the first right-hand corner, and immediately thereafter there is a tight left-handed curve. Everyone got through the first bend without difficulty but as we approached the second we could see a lot of debris in the middle of the circuit.

We wound our way around the larger fragments and saw that three cars had collided: de la Rosa in the Arrows, Nick Heidfeld in the Prost and Pedro Diniz in the Sauber. They had ended their race in a multiple shunt. We slowed down and had a look at Heidfeld, who was a bit slow to recover from the impact, but Diniz was all right and de la Rosa was getting out of his car. We pressed on hard and, despite the delay at this accident, we were well down the pit lane before the race leaders were charging down the pit-lane straight.

To my surprise, Hakkinen was in the lead, followed by Coulthard, with Schumacher in third position and Barrichello fourth. We were parked at the end of the pit lane in front of a huge TV screen so we could see clearly what was going on. The safety car had been brought out because of the first-lap accident but as the circuit was rapidly cleared of debris it was there for only one lap. The race resumed on the third lap and Hakkinen let Coulthard go by but Schumacher and Barrichello went past too. Then Hakkinen was brought in because he had jumped the start and had to do a ten-second penalty in his pit.

The leaders at this point were Coulthard, Schumacher and Barrichello, but as Ron Dennis told me later, Coulthard went off the circuit, filled one of his radiators with grass and was brought into the pit early. Immediately Schumacher set up a series of very fast laps, while Coulthard was going in and out of the pits, taking the lead with Barrichello second. When Schumacher came in for his pit stop, he exited in front of Coulthard in the classic way Ferrari have developed of maintaining their cars' positions by the speed and efficiency of their stops. Thereafter Coulthard kept in contact with Schumacher but was unable to overtake him, Barrichello was third, Hakkinen fourth. The drivers' points at the end of the race were Schumacher 108 and Hakkinen 89. In the Constructors' Championship, Ferrari ended with 170 to McLaren's 152.

Seven laps before the end of the race, we were horrified to see Johnny Herbert have a huge accident. The right rear wheel detached from his car and he spun at high speed, went laterally across the gravel pits and crashed heavily with the right side of the car into the tyre barrier. I was relieved to see him move immediately in the cockpit, and within a few seconds he was undoing his belts and taking off the steering-wheel. He got as far as the cockpit rim, but then it became clear that he was unable to use his legs to get out. The trackside marshals immediately went to him, extricated him and carried him through a gap in the circuit wall to an ambulance, which took him to the medical centre.

It was reported that he was only bruised, but as soon as the race ended we went to see how he was. He was grinning as happily as ever, and had damaged his left knee and ankle, but it seemed unlikely that anything was fractured. We X-rayed him, and confirmed that there was only soft-tissue damage although both the knee and the ankle were pretty painful. The consultant orthopaedic surgeon in the medical centre created splints for both joints. Johnny took it all cheerfully and said, 'Well, I limped into Formula One eleven years ago and I suppose I'm going to limp out of it now.' It was his last race for the Jaguar team and his last race in Formula One. His future career seems to lie in the CART series in the United States.

After everything had settled down in the medical centre I changed and went over to see Karl-Heinz Zimmerman for a glass of red wine. With him, I met Professor Jürgen Hubbert of the McLaren Mercedes team, who asked if I had seen David Coulthard. I had not, but I got hold of some of the team members to see what the problem was. Coulthard came over to see me in one of the air-conditioned offices and it appeared that the heat in his cockpit and the friction of his clothing had produced two contact areas on his rear end, one of which had blistered badly. I made some jocular remarks to the effect that he must have been urging his car on with his behind. But as it was of no great moment, he went away happily to join the McLaren Mercedes party, which was about to start.

The Ferrari team were over the moon, having walked away with fourteen points, and they had won the constructors' title comfortably for the tenth time. It was the first time for twenty-one years that the world championship title for driver and constructor had been won by Ferrari, and to quote Jean Todt, 'This dream result has been obtained thanks to a dream team.'

The fact that Schumacher had won four races in a row – Monza, Indianapolis, Suzuka and Kuala Lumpur – meant that, overall, he had won nine Grands Prix in 2000. As Barrichello had won one, Ferrari had been the victors in ten of the seventeen races. It was Schumacher's forty-fourth Grand Prix triumph, and his tally of nine races won in the season equalled his 1995 achievement with the Benetton team.

Of course, there was great relief all round that the season was over. The next day, as I sat alongside the swimming-pool at the Mandarin Oriental enjoying the wonderful view, I reflected that none of the drivers had been seriously hurt in 2000.

PART THREE

THE PERSONALITIES OF THE MILLENNIUM YEAR

MIKA HAKKINEN

Mika Hakkinen started 2000 as the world champion, and fought valiantly all year to retain his title. In 1996, still recovering from his 1995 head injury, he came third four times, fourth twice, fifth four times and sixth once – in other words, he was in the points eleven times in sixteen races.

In 1997 he won his first Grand Prix at Jerez, and was in the first six seven times. In 1998, two years after his injury,* he won eight Grands Prix, was second three times, in the first six places fourteen times in sixteen races – and won the world championship. Since winning the championship again in 1999, he has driven brilliantly and consistently, with a superb performance in the last race in Japan. He made an unforced error when leading in Monza, selecting the wrong gear at the second chicane. Immediately afterwards he broke down in tears, which, of course, the TV cameras recorded. The press made much of this breakdown.

---

* It is accepted in orthodox neurological practice that recovery from head injury may take up to two years to reach its maximum.

Most people do not realize the enormous mental and emotional effort these young men put into their performances. At one time it was not uncommon for a disappointed driver to throw a punch at marshals who were trying to be helpful. I remember James Hunt laying one on the chin of a marshal at Mosport in 1977 when the latter was trying to restrain him from running across the circuit. James was angry because he had been leading when he was pushed off the circuit by his McLaren team-mate, Jochen Mass, who was a lap down but came in third.

One one occasion when I was taking young Gianni Morbidelli in the medical car to the medical centre in Brazil after an accident in practice, he tried to jump out of the car and escape up the pit line. I grabbed his right wrist with my left hand, and he lowered his head and sank his teeth into my left hand. After that, he went straight to the medical centre as I was not amused.

In 1999 in Japan just before the race, I was walking up the pit lane looking at a motor-racing magazine. In it was a series of pictures of Hakkinen in tears and on his knees at Monza. I started to laugh. Suddenly I felt a presence in front of me.

'What are you laughing about?' Mika asked.

I decided to be honest. I showed him the photos and said, 'I hope we're not going to have any more nonsense like this.'

He grinned. 'Don't worry, I'll be gone like a flash at the start and nobody will catch me!' He did as promised, led for fifty of the fifty-three laps, won the race and the title.

MICHAEL SCHUMACHER

What more can be said of the wonderful talent of this young man? He is undeniably the quickest in the wet and the wiliest in the dry. I think he and Ayrton Senna were in the same class and, like Senna, Michael's ruthless determination to win, sometimes at all costs, gets him into trouble. He was in contention for the title in the last race of 1997 at Jerez and again in 1998 at Suzuka. He was out of luck in 1999 as a result of his accident at Silverstone. When he came back to race in Malaysia in 1999 he put his car on pole, and did the same at Suzuka. The millennium championship was his third title, adding to the two he won in 1994 and 1995 with Benetton.

I have always found Michael likeable, straightforward and pleasant to deal with, but many people complain that he is arrogant, particularly in the post-race TV interview. He is an extremely confident man and this, together with his manner when speaking English, is – in my view – mistaken for arrogance.

Michael has a dry, cynical wit: after his brother knocked him off the track at the start of the European Grand Prix at the first corner in 1997, he said of Ralf, 'He ought to see a psychiatrist and get some help.' Similarly, after Michael was damaged and pushed off by Zonta at the first corner at the start in Austria in 2000, he said, when asked about the incident, 'Zonta overestimated his own driving ability'.

He is a man who knows how to relax after a race, and on Sunday evening he likes to come to Karl-Heinz Zimmerman's motor-home for a beer and an occasional Havana cigar. Now, with forty-four Grand Prix wins to his credit at the age of thirty-two, he is in a position to challenge Alain Prost's all-time record of fifty-one wins and Fangio's record of five world championships.

DAVID COULTHARD

One of the nicest guys in the game, polite and well mannered, he has a great sense of humour and a cheeky grin. I first met David at Spa, at Jackie Stewart's request, when he was driving Formula Three for Jackie. David had had an accident on Sunday morning and had hurt his leg. He'd been seen in the medical centre, Jackie told me, and cleared, but was limping badly and the Formula One race was almost due to start. I hopped on the back of Jackie's scooter and went down to the old pits.

On examination, I thought he had probably fractured his fibula at the halfway mark. 'Didn't you get X-rayed in the medical centre?' I asked.

'Yes,' he replied, 'but they said it was normal.'

'Which leg did they X-ray?' I queried.

He thought for a few seconds and then, with a sheepish grin, said, 'The other one.'

Scottish innocence and Belgian technology clearly were not a good mix. He flew home with Jackie Stewart, the fracture was confirmed by X-ray and the leg put into a full-length below-knee plaster cast.

David rang me the next day to ask if this was really necessary and then came to see me with his X-rays. In fact, it was a simple fracture, without displacement mid-shaft, so I took the cast off and strapped his calf with Elastoplast support so that he could get back to racing in ten days' time without an immobilized ankle.

David seems to have most appalling luck in driving, and a full toss at the championship seems to evade him. His record is pretty good, though: in 107 Grand Prix starts, he has been first nine times, second twenty-one times, and third eleven times. In all, he has been in the top six places and in the points fifty-eight times.

I would like to see him come into his own over the next few years. He is a gentle soul, despite his forceful driving. Some years ago, he had just come second in a race when he said to Ron Dennis, 'Isn't it great I'm second?'

'No, second place means you're the first of the losers!' Ron replied.

JENSON BUTTON

Here is a new and unusual talent, and a remarkably relaxed young man. He has had a sensational season in his first year in Formula One, placed six times in the eleven races he completed, having been forced to retire in the other six. He outqualified Ralf Schumacher – who has much more experience – six times. For a rookie year, this is a pretty good result. Both Patrick Head and Gerhard Berger have told me that Jenson is a pleasure to work with, listens well and seems to have no hang-ups. He was on the same flight as me on the way back from Budapest on Monday after the Hungarian race and was suffering after a night on the town. Race day had been hot and I had been asked by ITV how much fluid a driver would lose in such conditions. Two litres per hour is the maximum sweat rate, I told them. On the plane I asked Button, as I like to call him, if he had felt the heat. He had, he said, and had lost three kilograms in weight. I gathered also that Mika Hakkinen, who had won, lost 3.5 kilograms.

In Japan this year, I was in the foyer of the hotel when Jenson and his dad came to check in at reception. Jenson was carrying some shirts and an electric iron. I asked them what the iron was for. Jenson's dad said, 'Jenson has to iron his own shirts.' I expressed surprise, and Jenson's dad said, 'He has to do it at home as well, it's not just for travelling.' So he hasn't been spoiled! He likes a good time, and at one stage was sporting a black eye which he had acquired, he said, 'In a disco' – when somebody's hand accidentally connected in the frenzy of the dance?

RUBENS BARRICHELLO

This plucky and likeable young man has great potential as well as great charm. My first real contact with him was at Donington in 1993 at the end of a very wet European Grand Prix in which Senna had excelled beyond all expectations. Rubens was in his car out on the circuit as Walter Robinson, my driver, and I circled the track at the end of the race. Rubens complained of cramp so I cheered him up by telling him that was one of Senna's complaints. After Ayrton's tragic accident in 1994 Rubens was very upset and I remember talking to him on a long flight later that year and he was still suffering. Rubens' own accident at Imola the same weekend as Senna's was, of course, frightening enough but added to that was his grief for his idol.

Prior to 2000, when he started to drive for Ferrari, he had accomplished a great deal despite these difficulties and in qualifying he had got himself on pole twice, and had been second in the race in Canada in 1995 with the Jordan car and in Monaco in 1997 with the Stewart team. He has been in the first six places in races twenty-eight times, not always in the most competitive cars. He has proved himself very quick in the wet – always a sign of great sensitivity in a driver as well as courage.

Driving for Ferrari in the millennium season he won at Hockenheim, and was second in four other races, third four times, fourth four times – thus being placed thirteen times out of seventeen races. In the other four races he did not finish. He was fourth in the Drivers' Championship with sixty-seven points. Jean Todt must be pleased with him.

It is very easy to pull his leg. Recently he grew himself a van Dyck beard I advised him he would be quicker if he shaved it off as he would be both more aerodynamic and lighter!

JOHNNY HERBERT

I shall miss Johnny Herbert's cheerful cheekiness around the circuits. It seems he is destined to go to the United States and race in CART. He had a wretched season in the Jaguar this year, failing to finish eight times; his best result was seventh in Austria. It seems he is never in the right car at the right time. Despite this, he has been in the top six places in twenty-nine races and won three Grands Prix. He is a good person and, at my request, served as patron of a small theatre and activity group for disabled youngsters in Kent, and despite his heavy schedule, he finds time to attend their productions. I firmly believe that his true potential as a Grand Prix driver was never realized.

EDDIE IRVINE

Here is one of the great characters of today's Formula One drivers. Eddie is extremely laconic and laid back, has a great sense of humour and a direct manner which does not always endear him to authority. I have to admit I have a soft spot for him and I would like to see him do really well. After Schumacher's accident in 1999 he performed brilliantly for Ferrari, winning four races, coming second twice, third three times, fourth twice, fifth once and sixth twice – finishing in the top six in seventeen races fourteen times. As a result he was second in the world championship with seventy-four points against Hakkinen's seventy-six.

In the millennium year, he struggled with the Jaguar car but remained good humoured and witty. Flying back from Japan a couple of years ago, I had a long chat with him during which I discovered he was living in Milan rather than Dublin, where I had thought he lived. When I asked him why, he shrugged his shoulders and said, 'I ran out of talent in Ireland so I thought I'd see what Italy could provide.'

JACQUES VILLENEUVE

I don't need to say anything about Jacques as a driver. He has a massive talent, as shown in his CART and Indianapolis successes and his performance in the Williams car in 1996, and again in 1997 when he won the championship and was on pole ten times. He is a really gutsy person with great character and determination. Sometimes his driving shows an optimism that is not based on any faith in the science of physics, but he is never deterred by this. On several occasions when I've mentioned to him that his efforts seemed to me over-enthusiastic, he has just grinned and said, 'You've got to go for it.' He has a penchant for dyeing his hair so one never knows what colour it is going to be – on the whole I prefer him blond!

THE OTHER MILLENNIUM DRIVERS

I do not know the younger drivers as well, personally, as those I have mentioned above. They are without exception a remarkable group – highly motivated, extremely fit and, for the most part, cheerful and outgoing. There is, of course, some exceptional talent, such as Ralf Schumacher, an indomitable performer, and naturally gifted drivers like Jarno Trulli and Giancarlo Fisichella, although the latter has seemed to go off tune since he had a spate of accidents including the inversion crash at Spa this year. Pedro de la Rosa and Mika Salo have great potential, as does Ricardo Zonta, who is at times, however, a little over-ambitious. Stalwarts like Jean

121

Alesi and Heinz-Harald Frentzen continue to do battle without much recent success and the solid Jos Verstappen persists gallantly in his efforts. Alexander Wurz and Nick Heidfeld have had disappointing seasons, and the newcomers Marc Gené and Gaston Mazzacane have tried hard in the Minardi team which, remarkably, seems to be surviving. I have always liked Pedro Diniz, who is a true gentleman in his personal relations and is so well mannered. I hope his move from driving to management brings him success – I know he doesn't need the money!

THE FIA MEDICAL CAR

The idea of having the same medical car and the same driver at every Grand Prix to follow the first lap was first mooted by Innes Ireland in February 1979, when we were together at the Hilton in São Paulo. In a brief paper, he pointed out the advantages of using the same powerful car with a properly trained driver who would know automatically what to do, thus eliminating the difficulty of training a new driver every other weekend into the routine and ritual, frequently with a language barrier. I showed the paper to Bernie, who said he thought it was a good idea but that we couldn't implement it yet. 'Anyway,' he said, 'Innes won't be allowed to drive you because he's very good at having accidents.'

Over the years I have had a variety of vehicles – including an ambulance which could get only to the first corner at Buenos Aires, trucks that got halfway round the circuit at Zolder, and a soft-top pink Porsche 911 at Spa. The last of these was most unsuitable because it rained all weekend. We started the race with about an inch of water on the circuit (there were no starts behind the safety car in those days – we didn't have a safety car), and slid all around the circuit on the first lap. The car was driven bravely by Michel Gilsoul and, fortunately, the Formula One cars were not so quick in the wet so we made it without incident. The thought of what might happen if an ordinary road soft-top was inverted when flat out on the circuit at Spa if I was wearing no protection save a crash helmet crossed my mind, but it didn't happen, thanks to Michel's skill.

Of course, I've had some great cars – a Ferrari Testarossa for one, driven by Frank Gardner at the first Adelaide race. After one lap, he pointed out that it had no brakes. I was in a slow, privately owned Mercedes, driven by Wilson Fittipaldi, at Rio when we were caught by the pack, having slowed up to look at Thierry Boutsen who had been having a moment. Of all the vehicles, including Fords, Peugeots, Alfa Romeos, Opels, Jaguars, Renaults, Audis, Hondas and Toyotas, I have favoured the Porsche 911, with or without turbo, though it is hard to cram an anaesthetist and the necessary equipment into the back. But for velocity and handling the 911 felt very comfortable to me. I didn't like the 928 so much, although the 944 was tolerable with Herbert Linge driving it. Exotic cars don't work too well, and in a Lamborghini, Jochen Mass and I shot down an escape road by the Hôtel Metropole in Monaco when we couldn't stop in the wet; we had to go into reverse to get back on to the circuit. One of the best trips round Monaco, with Jean-Pierre Jarier driving, was in a Renault turbo rally car – but there was little room for equipment and none for an anaesthetist.

I've had a few slides and spins in the hands of great drivers and others – Jacky Ickx at Monaco, Phil Hill at Long Beach, Vittorio Brambilla at Monza, someone unknown and best forgotten at Rivazza at Imola, another at the exit of Desado do Lago at Interlagos when I was on the way to rescue Nigel Mansell after an accident with Senna in final qualifying practice. In the main, though, I have been driven safely by all the above and by Carlos Reutemann, Andrea Montermini, Chico Serra, Derek Daly, Niki Lauda, Hector Rebaque, Raul Boesel, Rupert Keegan, Jan Lammers, Giovanni Lavaggi, Ricardo Zunino, Walter Robinson, Tim Evans, Gerry Gilbey, Bob Evans, Marc Duez, and many more.

Arturo Merzario was driving – Stetson and all – when we shot off to rescue Ukyo Katayama, who was off in the barrier at the Parabolica at Monza during afternoon practice in 1997. As we approached, Arturo said, 'Shall I drive across the gravel?'

'Sure,' I replied, 'if you can.'

We got halfway over before the Mercedes sank to its hubs, but at least Katayama didn't have to walk so far to reach us. Marlboro Man – Arturo – was not fazed: he just lit another Marlboro.

From the German ONS I have been looked after by Herbert Linge, Peter Lux, Jürgen Ditzinger, and recently at Nürburgring by a great chap called Herman. I didn't know his surname as we always called him Herman the German, but as well as being a great driver he kept me supplied with cigars. As did a fine young driver at Barcelona named Alfonso.

After Max Mosley formed a Formula One Safety Group in 1997 consisting of himself, Jean Todt, Bernie Ecclestone, Charlie Whiting, Damon Hill, Jacques Villeneuve, Mika Salo and me. After a meeting at Silverstone, a decision was made to recruit a permanent safety-car driver. Oliver Gavin was appointed and drove until the end of 1999.

Before June 1997, an arrangement had been made through the FIA, Bernie and Allsport Management, run by Paddy McNally, for Mercedes to supply safety cars to go to all Grands Prix worldwide. Two CLK 500s and two Mercedes 500 estates, together with six M cars turned up with tactful timing at the French Grand Prix to be used instead of the usual cars Renault had provided. This overturned the relationship we had with Renault, and Patrick Faure, chief of Renault Sport, got more than a bit cross.

About half an hour before the race I was in the paddock when Bernie appeared and called me over. 'Sid,' he said, 'I've got the chief of Renault Sport in my bus and he's very upset you did this deal with Mercedes. Will you come and explain it to him?' With consummate skill Bernie was sliding out of it.

I went in and told him the truth: 'In two recent years at Monaco, the Renault Laguna supplied to me was unsatisfactory. On one occasion the engine blew up going uphill from the start to Casino Square, and we had to coast from Casino Square down past Loews to find space to get off the circuit at the tunnel. On the next occasion the Laguna saloon had such poor grip in the wet we could not attempt to follow the first lap and had to pull off at the start at the pit exit. On that occasion, in 1996, Schumacher had had an accident before entering the tunnel. He was uninjured, but had he been hurt, I would not have been there as I had an unsuitable vehicle – a normal road saloon.' I added, 'The Renault Méganes supplied made a lot of noise but didn't go very fast.'

Patrick Faure was a bit upset and apologized, saying that

no such information had reached him or the problems would have been solved. I suggested perhaps there were some communication deficiencies in his staff. He asked if I would reconsider accepting Renaults if he promised to give us what we needed. Unfortunately, I replied, I could not as we now had a binding contract with Mercedes. We parted on friendly terms when I indicated I had to do the race – but I didn't tell him that my Mercedes 500 estate was waiting for me. Bernie showed me out and I asked, 'Was that OK, Bernie?' 'Good job,' he said and slapped me on the back.

For the last three seasons we have had wonderful cars. Of course, the medical car is not a normal Mercedes road car. It is fully Autrecht Melcher Grossapack (AMG) converted and has lowered suspension, special brakes and tyres and a five-litre-plus engine. It goes like a bomb. In the first two years we had an E body but for 1999 and 2000 we have had a C estate body so it is even faster. Ex-Formula One pilot Alex Ribeiro has been the driver, and with Gary Hartstein we are a good, happy medical team. At each Grand Prix we have an English-speaking anaesthetist or surgeon from the local medical team to avoid language problems with other circuit workers. We all know what to do when we get to an accident, and the driver knows the routine of medical inspections, safety-car practice and the ritual before and after the race. For the past several years Norbert Haug, the Mercedes race director, has asked me, 'Have you got all you want in the car?'

'Well,' I reply, 'we don't have a drinks cabinet or a humidor for our cigars.'

At a dinner at Monza in 2000, I told this story to Jürgen Schremp, the overall president of Daimler Mercedes Benz, who happens to like cigars too. When I arrived at the

Indianapolis circuit, Peter, the Mercedes engineer who looks after our cars, took me to the medical car with a big grin. He opened the compartment between the two front seats and pressed a button. Up popped a stainless-steel flask of whisky and a cedarwood block holding eight cigars in their tubes with the caps off – Montecristos, Cohibas, Romeo y Julieta, etc., but all Cuban. Surrounding this magnificent display was a cedarwood humidor with climate control and a relative humidity gauge. The caps had been taken off so that the humidity could reach the tobacco properly. Obviously the design was the work of a connoisseur, for a professional cigar-cutter and lighter completed the kit. As it was Thursday and there was no practice or race, I sampled the whisky – Glenmorangie! They had got everything right!

BERNIE ECCLESTONE

It is five years since I told Bernie I was writing a book (*Life at the Limit*, 1996, Macmillan) that would include some comments about him. He threatened to sue me if I wrote anything nice about him. I sent him a copy of the manuscript, to which he made one correction. I had said that the Brabham fan car had been banned, but Bermie pointed out that in fact it had been withdrawn – so it could not be classed as banned. His mind is precise, acute and succinct. I was recently in a meeting with him when controversy was raging about agreeing the date of a future meeting. An enormous amount of time was wasted. In the end Bernie put his hand up and said, 'Mr Chairman, I can suggest a date.'

'And what date would that be?'

'April the first, All Fool's Day,' said Bernie. 'Before noon.'

In all the twenty-two years I have worked for and with him, he has been a staunch supporter of both safety and me. This does not mean that he hesitates to take the mickey out of me. One of his favourite ploys when I ring him or he rings me is to adopt a heavy foreign accent. On one occasion when my wife answered the phone, she failed to recognise him. When she asked him the purpose of his call, he replied, 'It's not your business.' Eventually, when he'd wound her up sufficiently, he said calmly, 'Susan, it's Bernie!'

In Austria this year, on race morning, I was struck down by what was probably a salmonella infection and felt a bit light-headed and sick. Gary Hartstein and Jean-Jacques Isserman brought the cardiac monitors to Bernie's motor-home where I was resting. They put on all the electrodes for a full electrocardiogram while Bernie watched with interest and an air of amusement. Before they had analysed the result – which was negative, as I expected – Bernie had taken them aside and said, 'If he's dead take him out, covered up, but tell everybody it's me. I'll hide for the rest of the day – but I'll turn up at the office tomorrow morning!'

Some years ago, just before I was due to leave for Japan, an old friend rang up unexpectedly. He said, 'Tell Sid *not* to go to Japan as he will be killed there.' My friend went on to explain that, since we had last seen him, he'd become psychic, could predict the future and had had a manifestation about me. My wife, who took the call, handed the telephone to me and I duly heard him out, including his prediction that speed would kill me. I thanked him profusely for his advice and concern, then explained that, even with a potentially fatal outcome, I could not avoid going. However, Susan, full of anxiety, decided to come with me, and next morning we set off. On the Sunday morning of the race, I was chatting to Bernie after the warm-up. Suddenly he said, 'I was suprised to see Susan at the official dinner last night. She doesn't normally come to Japan.' I explained the background. Bernie grinned. 'She shouldn't have worried – I'd have made sure we got the body back. After all, we've got plenty of containers and we could slide you into one of those!'

In 1999 when he needed a coronary artery bypass operation, his sense of humour didn't let him down. I arranged for him to be looked after by Peter Mills, a superb caridologist, and operated upon by John Wright, a brilliant cardiac surgeon at the London Chest Hospital. At Bernie's request we made it a low-profile affair. I delayed my departure for the Canadian Grand Prix so that I could be in London on the day of the surgery. All went well, and I left for Canada on 9 June, travelling via the USA as I was lecturing at Wayne State University in Michigan that Wednesday night. When I got to the Montreal circuit on Thursday, many people asked me where Bernie was and, in particular, Martin Whitaker, chief of the Ford racing team, which was supplying engines to the Stewart team. I was more than sparing with the truth in telling everybody he'd gone to China to fix up a Grand Prix there! The next morning I rang the hospital to see how Bernie was, and was told that he was doing fine. The nurse at the other end said they were having trouble with his sense of humour – they didn't know when to take him seriously. Apparently, on the day after the operation two nurses, one each side of his bed, were adjusting the vacuum pressures in the drains from the chest and seemed to be having trouble. Bernie watched this for some minutes then said, 'You seem to be having trouble with that equipment – would you like me to get out of bed and help you, girls?' One of the nurses rushed off to phone John Wright to tell him that Mr Eccle-stone was confused or brain-damaged. 'Don't worry,' came back the reply. 'It's only his sense of humour.' Bernie went home on the fifth post-operative day and appeared at Silver-stone on 9 July, a month after the operation.

On 16 June, through the FIA, Bernie had issued the following press release. Please note the cautionary note, which appears in brackets, for all of his adversaries or pretenders to his throne.

> FIA Vice President Bernie Ecclestone has had a suc-cessful coronary artery bypass graft operation carried out by Consultant Cardiac Surgeon Mr John Wright and his team at the London Chest Hospital.
>
> Before discharging Bernie from hospital today, Mr Wright described the operation as 'routine' and said, 'Bernie will be back in the fast lane in a couple of weeks.'
>
> Bernie was urged to have the operation by his wife Slavica and by FIA Medical Chief Professor Watkins, who feared he might otherwise have to carry it out himself in the Medical Centre at a Formula One Race.
>
> (Note: Jean-Marie Balestre, Honorary President of the FIA and current President of the FIA Senate, had the same operation in 1986.)*

---

* This is code for 'I'll be around for at least another thirteen years' – so watch out everybody!

PART FOUR

THE 'GOLDEN OLDIES'

JIM CLARK

Jim Clark was the quietest Formula One driver I have ever known. Even on the night after he had clinched his first world championship in 1963, having won the Italian Grand Prix at Monza, he was quiet, composed and polite. When he joined Dean Delamont, then head of the RAC Motor Sport Division, and me at dinner at the Hôtel de Ville in Monza Park he excused himself early to go to bed, escaping the shenanigans that erupted as the triumphant Lotus team and the BRM team started to pelt each other with bread rolls. Saucers and plates followed, and then some live-wire spotted the tank of trout swimming around waiting to be selected for somebody's supper. A few fish joined the fray, and then the opposition got into the lobster tank at the other end of the room. When the hotel management staff stepped in it was time to leave . . .

I'd seen Jim Clark drive at Silverstone and Aintree in 1960 and 1961 and his driving was marked by extraordinary precision when, lap after lap, it seemed he could clip the same blades of grass – no Armco safety barriers in those days – as he cornered apparently effortlessly. In 1962 he had won the Belgian and British Grands Prix. In October that year I joined the Watkins Glen medical team and witnessed Jim winning the US Grand Prix. In August he had been fourth at the German Grand Prix at Nürburgring when, in appalling weather, the start of the race had been delayed because of a landslide on to the circuit. The next day Dean Delamont and I returned to the UK with Jim's prize money under the back seat of Dean's Wolsley car (with a Coventry Climax engine). Graham Hill had won the race, despite his terrifying accident in practice when a camera came off Carel Godin de Beaufort's car, and the debris destroyed Hill's Lotus. I remember Graham's posture as he sat on the floor of his pit in pouring rain, looking as miserable as sin. After he won he cheered up, and at the prize-giving dinner began his speech with characteristic humour by calling the audience to order with a loud *'Achtung.'*

The combination of Jim Clark and Colin Chapman brought the championship for Jim in 1963 with seven Grand Prix wins in ten races, and in 1965 with six wins in nine races. Out of seventy-two Grand Prix races in eight seasons, he won twenty-five times, and in 1965 he also won the Indianapolis 500. He won the Belgian Grand Prix at Spa four times in a row – 1962, 1963, 1964 and 1965.

Jim Clark came from Duns in the Borders where, strangely enough, the vet who looked after the animals on his father's farm was the father of fellow racing driver Innes Ireland. In the late eighties when I moved to the Borders, Jim's early racing practice on the deserted roads up there was legendary. The locals took shelter when he was about! Coincidentally, ghillie Jim Mitchell, with whom I fished the Tweed at Lord Home's beat at Birgham, had fished with Jim Clark on the same beat, and our inherited gardener Jock

Howie had attended Jim Clark's funeral. Jim had gone to school at Loretto, where my stepsons were educated, and the school chapel displays a memorial plaque to him.

It was a great shock to learn of the fatal accident at Hockenheim in April 1968; the cause is still unknown. I was at a neurosurgical conference in Chicago, where the civil rights riots and fires were in progress, when I heard the bad news.

PHIL HILL

Phil Hill is one of my favourite people. I didn't meet him until the Long Beach Grand Prix in April 1979 but I had long admired and respected him. When I became fascinated with Grand Prix racing after I returned to the UK from Africa in 1956, Juan Manuel Fangio and Stirling Moss dominated the sport. Fangio won the world championship for the fourth and fifth times in 1956 and 1957. In 1958 I was working at the Radcliffe Infirmary, Oxford, and able to escape to Silverstone, where Moss put the Vanwall on pole, but Peter Collins won the race for Ferrari – he was killed in the next race, at Nürburgring. Meanwhile, Phil Hill had been driving sports cars for Ferrari, winning Le Mans in 1958, and was now brought into the official Ferrari team for the Italian Grand Prix at Monza alongside Mike Hawthorn. His performance was spectacular: he led the race for most of the way, getting the fastest lap and finishing third to Mike Hawthorn's second. The next month, at Casablanca for the Moroccan Grand Prix, he was again in third place behind Hawthorn in second.

The next year, 1959, he was fourth in the world championship behind Jack Brabham, Tony Brooks and Stirling

Moss. In 1960 he won his first Grand Prix in Italy and also made the fastest lap. He was third at Monaco, and fourth at Spa – it was the weekend during which Chris Bristow and Alan Stacey were killed. He was fifth in the world championship with 'Taffy' von Trips, his team-mate, sixth.

In 1961 I remember seeing Phil and von Trips at the British Grand Prix at Aintree when Phil took pole. Taffy von Trips won the race and Phil came second. That year was remarkable for Ferrari: at the Italian Grand Prix, Hill and von Trips were in contention for the title, Hill with twenty-nine points and von Trips with thirty-three, with von Trips on pole. That day I was visiting my sister in the Wye valley when news came through on the radio of an appalling accident: Taffy had been killed after an incident on the second lap on the banked circuit when he and Jim Clark were thought to have touched. Phil went on to win the race and the world championship. Twenty years later, Enzo Ferrari invited Phil to drive the medical car at the Dino Ferrari circuit – named after Ferrari's son – at Imola.

I first saw Phil at close quarters at the Sebring race in 1963, when my entrance ticket positioned me over the Ferrari pit for the endurance race. I noticed then how energetic, quick-moving and vibrant he was – always talking, gesticulating and walking restlessly about the pit. By then he was an accomplished sports-car driver and had won the Le Mans twenty-four-hour race three times. When we met in 1979 my first impressions were reinforced: he was immediately friendly, intelligent and articulate, and had an irreverent sense of humour that matched mine. We became good friends, and at Indianapolis in 2000 he told me that I was one of *his* favourite people!

Phil drove me at Long Beach in 1979, 1980, 1981, 1982

and 1983, and in 1981 in Las Vegas and Imola. It was always exciting because he was so quick at the start – we had to be particularly careful at Long Beach, when the Formula One cars queued up to take the chicane at the end of Shoreline Drive, that we didn't get among the back markers. On one occasion, just before the start at Long Beach, he asked me if I was nervous, to which I replied, 'No.' With a laugh, he said, 'You bastard, you do this every two weeks and I only do it once a year.' Nevertheless, he did it rather well.

He turns up at some of the European races and always at Monza, and seeks me out in the medical car at the pit exit. When we can we retire to Karl-Heinz Zimmerman's motorhome for a chat or, after the practice, a glass of red wine. When things are quiet, I sometimes steal a lap or two round the Monza circuit with Phil at the wheel of the medical car. He likes to recount tales of severe vibration in the old Formula One cars taking the Curva Grande and the Lesmos corners, and the sensation of going in and out of the old banked circuit, which has a terrifyingly steep angle. It is tough even to walk up the banking – I have tried to do it. This year at Monza he described to me his experiences in the Two Worlds Trophy in 1958, when the Indy roadsters competed against European cars. To accommodate the Indy cars, the race had to be run in the opposite direction, anticlockwise rather than clockwise, so entering and leaving the banked circuit for the road course was rather more difficult.

In his book *Motor Racing Today* (1961) Innes Ireland described Phil initially as introspective, nervous, a worrier – but then went on to say that he was also sincere, had a cool nerve, was determined and possessed a wry sense of humour. I second that!

STIRLING MOSS

I never knew Stirling Moss when he was racing, and it is only in the years since I started to work for Bernie Ecclestone that I have come into contact with him and we have become friends. I remember the first time I saw him driving a car. It was when I was in training at Oxford, that I went to Silverstone and saw the magnificent sight of Stirling driving an Aston Martin DB4, drifting it through the old Woodcote corner. This corner was a wonderful spot to watch the cars. It has been completely changed in accordance with modern Grand Prix requirements. Looking at that corner today, you cannot imagine the thrills of the past. To me, and most other young men in the UK in the late fifties and sixties, Stirling was a hero.

One of the great moments I witnessed occurred when the British Grand Prix was run at Aintree and Stirling was barrelling up the straight into the final corner before the grandstands and the finish line. It had been raining torrentially, and the circuit was slippery. As he came into the corner to start to brake, he spun 360 degrees, caught the car as its nose pointed in the right direction and continued on his way round the corner. With bated breath, I waited for him to come round the next time and wondered if he would take it a bit slower, but he came in just as quickly, this time without losing control, receiving a tremendous cheer and applause from the crowd; he lifted his left hand in acknowledgement, and continued down the pit straight.

When I got to know him I discovered what tremendous fun he is. In the late fifties I had seen this side of his character at a race in Silverstone when he and Innes Ireland were driving Minis. When the flag dropped, Innes Ireland and Stirling were on the front row. They went backwards for a while through the pack, then set off in pursuit. Of course, they caught everyone else and finally won the race. However, having taken the flag at the start–finish line in front of the stands they proceeded to do a series of handbrake spins to the great delight of the crowd. Naturally, they were called before the stewards of the race and got a good ticking-off.

I was a spectator at Goodwood, early in 1962, on the awful day when Stirling had the accident that ended his career as a Formula One driver. When the race was stopped, there was silence in all of the grandstands while it was announced that he had crashed and been injured. We were all cheered when we heard via the PA system that his condition was satisfactory and that he had sent a message to his mother not to worry about him. Later that day, though, we realized the seriousness of his injuries when it was announced that he had been admitted to the neurosurgical unit at the Atkinson-Morley Hospital, that he was unconscious and had serious weakness in his arm and leg. Eventually Mr Wylie McKissock, the consultant neurosurgeon looking after Stirling, tired of the press attention he and his team were attracting and announced publicly that Stirling Moss had been badly injured, that he would never again drive a racing car and that there would be no further announcements from the hospital.

Some time after that we were told that Stirling was making a good recovery, and later that year he came to a race at Oulton Park in Cheshire. He arrived by helicopter and walked across the circuit to the cheers of the crowd. In the previous year he had won races at Monte Carlo and at

Nürburgring. During his career, in which he started in sixty-six Grands Prix, he won sixteen, was second five times and third twice. He had sixteen pole positions, thirty-seven front-row starts and made the fastest lap twenty times. He was never world champion but he came second in the championship four years in a row, three times behind Fangio and once behind Mike Hawthorn.

I gather that after his injury he tried testing again but felt himself too much off the pace to continue. Eventually he came back to race in other series. I believe that he made his practice attempts six months after his injury; in neurosurgical terms that was probably too soon for him to have recovered to the level of his original ability. Two of the most discerning motor-racing writers, Nigel Roebuck and Maurice Hamilton, have placed Stirling Moss as number one in the top ten drivers of all time.

I heard from Dean Delamont, who knew Stirling well, that he loved gadgets. After receiving an invitation to dinner from Stirling and his wife Susie at his flat, I was interested to see how true this was. One gadget in particular impressed me: a gigantic electrically driven pepper mill, with a searchlight attached to the bottom so that you could see the speed and extent of the peppering. I liked it so much that eventually I was given one, which I still enjoy using.

I – and I believe probably everyone else in the UK – was delighted for Stirling when he was knighted in the New Year Honours of 2000.

INNES IRELAND

I first met Innes Ireland at a little coffee shop in Watkins Glen in the early sixties. I had seen him in action on the track at Silverstone, Goodwood and Aintree, and I admired him as a courageous driver and, also, as an adventurous man; the details of some of his escapades had been related to me by Dean Delamont. Innes was the son of a vet but, although highly intelligent and articulate, he was not given to study and became fascinated at an early age with motor cars.

Once when Innes was at Aintree he was sitting on the grid surrounded by people, some of whom were rather good-looking ladies. He always had an eye for a good-looking bird, and on this occasion, even though the race was about to start, he was doing his best to establish a close relationship with one.

Much later on he told me that one night he had gone to dinner in a hotel where the restaurant's ornate ceiling was supported by huge pillars. Sitting alone at his table, he caught sight of a good-looking lady on the other side of the room. Her table was partly obscured by a pillar but she appeared to be alone. Innes called over a waiter, scribbled a note and asked him to take it to her. It read, 'If you would like to make love with me, please turn and smile.' It would be hard not to turn and smile at a note such as that, and she did. Then Innes saw a huge hand appear from behind the pillar and take the note from her. A few moments later a man – Innes described him as seven feet tall and weighing three hundred pounds – marched purposefully to his table and demanded an apology, which Innes said, 'I was very agreeable to give, having witnessed his size and strength.'

139

One year in Sebring, I think it was 1963, Innes had been offered a lift out in a private plane. He accepted, and found himself with a problem: he had a Hertz rental car, which he had picked up when he arrived, and which he had to return. In those days, the Hertz slogan ran, 'Pick it up here, drop it there and we'll take care of it.' Innes decided to put this to the test. He drove the car across the hotel lawn and at the last moment slipped out to watch it plunge into the swimming-pool. He then called Hertz: 'I picked it up in Miami and I've dropped it in the swimming-pool at the Sebring Motel.' When they came to pick up the car, Hertz brought a television crew and hauled it out with a crane, the slogan prominently on display. Innes was a little aggrieved when I told him that this incident had formed the basis of a Hertz TV advertising campaign and said ruefully, 'And I didn't get a bloody penny for it.'

After he retired from motor racing, he took up journalism and wrote a book about his early years called *All Arms and Elbows*, an account of the many accidents he had and the remarkable recoveries he made afterwards. His idea of rehabilitation was a novel one and consisted largely of cigarettes and whisky.

We enjoyed many good dinners together around the world while he was writing for *Road and Track*. One night in São Paulo we had so much fun that on race morning, when I went to collect Innes from his bedroom, he said he could not get out of bed and come to the circuit. He asked me to pay close attention to what happened that day and return to his room as soon as possible after the race to tell him about it. Then he would type up his copy and send it off to the journal.

He was immensely proud of having won the first United States Grand Prix at Watkins Glen for Team Lotus in 1961, and upset when shortly afterwards Colin Chapman fired him. Thereafter he found it difficult to get a competitive drive. He had been second in other races twice and third once, fourth in four Grands Prix, fifth in four others and sixth in two. In view of his immense courage and driving style it was surprising that he was not more successful, but he had a lot of accidents. Some years later he wrote in my copy of *All Arms and Elbows*: 'Shit, I wish I'd known you twenty years earlier when I would have needed you more often.'

Naturally, he fancied himself as a fast driver on the road. On one occasion when we were leaving the Formula One car park in the middle of the paddock at Spa, after the race, he said to me, 'What ferry are you on?'

'The eight o'clock,' I replied.

'So am I, see you there.'

He led the way, taking the usual route out of the circuit, which leads through heavily congested car parks and some small villages to a long queue for the motorway. I had worked out how to avoid this by driving around the circuit to the medical centre, exiting on to a country road, passing Liège before joining the motorway to Calais. Consequently I arrived in good time for the eight o'clock ferry – I was driving a Porsche 911 – and sat almost at the head of the queue to board. About twenty minutes later, Innes came ambling down the queue of cars. He looked absolutely astonished to find me nearly at the head of the queue and said, 'How the fuck did you get here so quick?'

'I just drove at my normal pace, Innes.'

'Well, there's no way you could have overtaken me.'

'So how did I get here twenty minutes ahead of you?'

I never let him in on the secret, and his nose was a bit out of joint about this, so I invited him to dinner and we had our usual fun on the ferry, although he kept shaking his head in a puzzled way.

When we got off the ferry at Dover, he set off hell for leather, heading up the motorway to London, and I tucked in behind him. Despite all his best efforts, he couldn't shake me off.

Some years later he came up to Belmont, my home in Scotland, as he was to address the motor-racing club of Loretto School at Musselburgh. When we left the house, we got into my Jaguar XJS V12. 'I hope you're going to drive this carefully,' Innes said, to which I replied, 'Naturally,' and I did.

We got to the school and had dinner with the boys. Then Innes got up to make a speech in which he was uproariously funny in recounting episodes from his racing days that I had not heard before. Later that night over whisky in my sitting room, he told me that he was having health problems and, as he put it, 'the dreaded lurgy' had got him. I was immensely sad when I was told at the Japanese Grand Prix in 1993 that Innes had died of cancer a few days before.

JACKIE STEWART

There were two people in the world – apart from family – who would ring me up when they needed nothing: Ayrton Senna and Jackie Stewart. Usually telephone calls to me carry an agenda, either overt or covert, but this pair would ring me up just to say hello. They shared other attributes: precision of thought and action, overpowering dedication to their sport, incredible driving ability, ambition and, apparently, fearlessness in a Grand Prix car.

In 1973 I went to Monaco with Valentine Logue, my old chief in neurosurgery, with whom I trained and did research at the Middlesex and Maida Vale Hospital for Nervous Diseases, in London. We went on a Page & Moy package, and stayed at the Metropolitan Hotel. Our seats for the qualifying practices were in Casino Square, directly opposite the point where the Formula One cars entered it – so that they were pointing directly at the stand as they accelerated through the area. I remember the terrifying speed at which Jackie came through in practice, driving a Tyrrell Ford with François Cevert, his team-mate, on his tail. Jackie put the car on pole.

Similarly, on race day, as we sat alongside the Royal Box on the pit straight, he went belting past, heading for St Dévote and for victory in the race. François Cevert was fourth. Jackie had already been world champion in 1969 and 1971, winning six Grands Prix in each of these years. In 1973 he won five races, and had two second places, one third place, two fourth and two fifth places – in other words, he was in the points in twelve of the fourteen Grands Prix in which he drove. He did not drive in the last – the fifteenth – race at Watkins Glen in October: the team and he withdrew because of François Cevert's fatal accident in practice. Nevertheless, he was world champion again.

Cevert had the most beautiful and hypnotically blue eyes I have ever seen in a man. He was an extrovert, wont to empty his bladder in front of the grandstand just before the start of the race – he did this at Silverstone in 1973: there were cheers from the men and gasps from the ladies as he unzipped his fly. His death had a profound effect on Jackie, as did so many of the other tragedies in the sixties and seventies. Jackie told me later that he had already resolved earlier that year to retire at the end of the season, but the accident confirmed his decision.

Ken Tyrrell, for whom Jackie drove, told me that Jackie's outstanding feature as a racing driver was his extreme sensitivity to a car, its balance, handling and performance. He would bring it in during testing and make some comment or complaint. The fault would frequently take time to identify, but he was usually right. Ken told me that in one of the Monaco races Jackie had lost his rear brakes on the parade lap, but carried on regardless and went the whole race, on that particularly tortuous circuit, with sensational throttle control and delicate braking. I remember his intense concentration while he was sitting in the car before he set off in practice or for the race: he would stare into space, oblivious to all that was going on around him, his face blank.

Although I'd met him at Watkins Glen in the sixties, and at Silverstone in the seventies, I only got to know him, as a friend, after I started working for Bernie Ecclestone in 1978 as FOCA's (Formula One Constructors' Association) surgeon. Since then, he has been immensely helpful to me and has supported me wholeheartedly on safety issues. He has an irrepressible sense of humour, a ready wit – against which you have to guard yourself – and an inexhaustible fund of anecdotes. He loves to tell the story of his accident in the wet at Spa in 1966, when he lay unconscious, trapped in his BRM. Graham Hill got him out, took off Jackie's overalls and his underwear as they were soaked in petrol, then went for help.

Waking up, Jackie found that he was attended by three nuns, the first of whom said she hadn't known a man had such a thing, the second that she knew but had never seen one, the third that she had seen one but never so enormous. Presumably they were speaking in French or Flemish and I assume that Jackie is a better linguist than I'd thought he was. Nevertheless, for his sixtieth birthday, I had made and framed an appropriate card depicting three nuns leaping over a recumbent, conscious and proud – in more ways than one – Jackie Stewart with a self-satisfied expression on his face. He wrote to thank me for my gift and claimed it did not do him justice!

For several years we have worked together for charities, fund-raising for the College of Occupational Therapists, for Alzheimer's disease, for the Grand Prix Mechanics Trust, and for the British Brain and Spine Foundation, among others. Jackie has played in nearly every Grand Prix Drivers' Golf Day, held after Silverstone, for the British Brain and Spine Foundation with his son Paul. He is an excellent golfer, as, indeed, many Formula One drivers are: Jacques Lafitte, Jackie Oliver, Damon Hill, John Watson, Martin Brundle, David Coulthard, Nigel Mansell, Mika Hakkinen, Eddie Irvine and Johnny Herbert have all turned out at my request and we've always had a lot of fun.

In June 2000 Jackie and I were invited to a cross-country event to proffer advice about safety as a result of the appalling death rate in cross-country eventing in the previous year. Nine riders had been killed worldwide as a result of horses falling and landing on their riders. We went to the Branham event, and afterwards made our views known to the establishment concerning fences, protective hats and body armour.

We hope, fervently, that changes will be made not only to protect the professionals and expert riders but to reduce the morbidity and mortality in youngsters growing up in the sport. After forty-two years as a neurosurgeon, when I am asked what I consider the most dangerous sport I have to say, 'Horses – in all their forms.'

JACK BRABHAM

I first met Jack Brabham in 1962 when I was with Dean Delamont and we were having dinner in a restaurant near Adenau at Nürburgring. Jack came over and started pinching our chips. He had already been world champion in 1960, when he had won Grands Prix in Holland, Belgium, France, the UK and Portugal. In the previous year, 1959, he had also been world champion. In those days he drove for Cooper Climax but in 1962 he was at the wheel of a Brabham Climax.

Jack is a wonderfully nonchalant character, who drove in Formula One from 1955 until the end of the season in 1970. Dean Delamont knew him well and told me anecdotes of Jack's legendary calm. He described an occasion when Jack was landing his aeroplane and discovered that the brakes were not working properly. As he swept down the rain-sodden runway it seemed that he was going to run out of road, but he performed one of his motor-racing tricks and spun the aeroplane so that it halted well within the limits of the runway. Apparently he got out of the plane without comment, as he had on another occasion. This time Dean was with him in a road car when Jack lost control, went through

146

a hedge and ended up in a field. He got out and walked away without a word.

In 1966 he won the world championship again, in a Brabham Repco, the first driver ever to win it in a car of his own construction. That year he also won four Grands Prix in France, Great Britain, Holland and Germany. He was on the front row of the grid thirty-eight times in his career and won pole position thirteen times.

I have seen him quite a lot since he retired from Grand Prix racing for he regularly turns up at Silverstone and in Australia, of course, and elsewhere. He and Frank Gardner are very good friends, so I always hear from one about the other, and I last saw him in Suzuka when he was looking forward to Frank's forthcoming seventieth birthday party.

Of course, since he retired from racing he has continued to drive fast cars in demonstrations at circuits and, indeed, in occasional races. In the Goodwood Revival Meeting in 1999 when racing Jackie Oliver, he had a big accident which left him unconscious with injuries to his chest and spine. On the night of the event Jackie Stewart telephoned to tell me about the accident, and I spoke to the surgeon looking after Jack and was reassured he would be OK. When I met Jack in Australia in 2000 I asked him if he had recovered fully from his accident. 'I've had another big shunt since then,' he said cheerfully, but fortunately he had escaped injury.

GRAHAM HILL

Graham Hill was one of the wittiest men ever in Grand Prix racing and an accomplished after-dinner speaker, rivalling Jackie Stewart. The two of them liked to do a double-act, taking the mickey out of each other. I remember Graham interrupting Jackie, who was in full flow, one night and advising him to stand up when he was making a speech. 'I'm already standing on my toes,' Jackie replied. When celebrating Graham was given to taking off his trousers and climbing on the table – to roars of applause and badinage.

He attended a seminar on motor-racing medicine at the Royal Society of Medicine in London during the early sixties, in which I participated. After listening seriously to our accounts of blood pressure, pulse rate and temperature changes, he brought down the house in the lecture theatre by enquiring gently about the physiological effects of the crotch strap, which, he averred, he disliked as it had an adverse effect on his libido. A likely story, the audience thought.

He had a long career in Formula One – from 1958 to 1975 and competed in 176 Grands Prix. He was on the first row of the grid forty-two times and was in the points in sixty Formula One races. Of these he won fourteen, was second fifteen times and third seven times. He was world champion in 1962 and 1968. He won the Monaco Grand Prix five times, and the Indianapolis 500 in 1966. In those days, Grand Prix drivers did not confine themselves only to For- mula One races and it was a great joy for spectators in the UK to see Stirling Moss, Innes Ireland, Jim Clark, Roy

Salvadori and, of course, Graham competing in sports cars and saloons. It was a particular pleasure to see big Jaguars sliding round the original Woodcote corner at Silverstone in the hands of those doyens of motor racing. In 1972 Graham, aged forty-three, won Le Mans.

I remember Graham's composure at Watkins Glen in 1965, when he was thirty-six, and a young Scot, Jackie Stewart, aged twenty-six, had just joined BRM and had recently won at Monza, with Graham in second place. Jackie was trying to wind him up by proclaiming in the pits, 'I'm a better driver than you, Graham Hill.' Graham got pole position and won the race.

Towards the end of his long career, when he and Jack Brabham were slipping backwards down the grid, Graham commented, 'There's a nicer class of people at our end of the grid, Jack.'

In October 1969 he had a bad accident, fracturing his legs, at Watkins Glen, but struggled to be fit enough to race in South Africa at Kyalami the next March. He was sixth in the race despite pain in his legs. In 1975 he retired from driving and took up running his own Embassy team, with Tony Brise as his driver. Tragically, in November 1975, his plane crashed when he was attempting to land in bad weather after returning with Brise and the team from the Paul Ricard circuit in France where they had been testing.

JODY SCHECKTER

Ayrton Senna apart, the driver to whom I was closest was, and is, Jody Scheckter. After he retired, in 1980, and went to live in the USA, I saw less of him, but he turned up at the occasional Grand Prix and came to the pit exit to pull my leg.

I always thought he was smart to retire when he did at the age of thirty and to make a successful life away from motor sport. Now, his sons are in the game, and I saw him at the Grands Prix in 2000, with Tomas driving in Formula 3000. I think it was in Spa that Tomas had a couple of excursions into the gravel, in practice and in the race. When my medical car picked him up, he said he wasn't looking forward to hearing what his father would have to say to him. I gave him some ammunition: I described the occasion at Monza in 1978, when Jody destroyed the Armco at Lesmo on the parade lap of the second start so heavily that the third attempt to start was very late and the race had to be shortened to finish before dark . . .

In my earlier book, *Life at the Limit*, I stated that Jody Scheckter had caused an accident in the 1973 British Grand Prix at Woodcote corner, Silverstone, and included a picture of him captioned: '. . . looking as if he is about to cause trouble (which he frequently did in and out of the car!)'. The lawyers wanted me to take out these remarks, but instead I rang Jody and told him what I'd said about him. Typical Jody answer: 'If you said that about me, Professor, it's got to be right.' I then told him that the lawyers thought it actionable; you can imagine what he said about them!

His greatest year was 1979 when he was driving for Ferrari

with Gilles Villeneuve as his team-mate. Jody clinched the championship by winning the Italian Grand Prix at Monza, and Gilles was second. Italy was in raptures.

Jody had driven his first Grand Prix for McLaren in 1972 at Watkins Glen. He drove in 112 races, and was in the top six places fifty-three times – a remarkably consistent perform-ance, including ten wins and thirty-three podium positions. At the beginning of his career I wondered if he would survive the course but, increasingly mature, his consistency in the top six places paid off.

He was pretty quick in a road car, too, and I remember an epic trip from Long Beach to Los Angeles airport on the Monday after the 1980 race. That morning I'd been to the hospital to see Clay Regazzoni, and we set off a little late to make the flight. Approaching Los Angeles there was a huge traffic jam but, undaunted, Jody took the soft shoulder and went past miles of traffic. We caught the flight, and his only worry seemed to be that the soft-shoulder debris might have caused a puncture.

I will always be grateful to him for support on safety issues when he was president of the Grand Prix Drivers' Assocation. Its meetings, which I attended, were pretty noisy, with Jody, Didier Pironi and Eddie Cheever in full voice. At one meeting in South Africa, I was asked to recruit Professor Christiaan Barnard to the medical team and had to explain that as he was world famous we couldn't afford his fees, even if he could afford the time for three days of practice and the race.

Jody was always great in the drivers' briefings on the Sunday mornings after the warm-up. When contentious points came up, he was always direct. The ego of more than one Clerk of the Course was punctured and his self-image shattered after a brief encounter with Jody's eloquence and pungency.

MARIO ANDRETTI

One of the nicest gestures ever made to me in recognition of my work in motor sport was by Mario Andretti when he nominated me for the Mario Andretti Award for Excellence in Medicine. I had a call from the nominating panel asking me to come to Detroit in 1996 to receive it at a ceremony at the Yacht Club preceding the CART race that weekend on Belle Isle. I collected a beautiful silver Paul Revere bowl, suitably inscribed, and made a speech in response to Mario's, teasing him a little in the way I know he likes. Then he drove us to dinner at an excellent restaurant. He was still driving competitively at that time – as he demonstrated on the way to dinner.

I have always liked Mario – from the moment I met him at Brands Hatch in the control tower in 1978; Bernie Ecclestone had invited me to meet the Formula One drivers when I was appointed FOCA's surgeon. Mario is a great ambassador for motor sport – thoughtful, eloquent, smooth and polished; his politeness and excellent manners are charming. However, he can also produce language that would make a trooper faint. I first saw him on TV driving in the Indy 500; when his car failed he got out and kicked it. He strongly denies this, so maybe my memory is failing. But what a driver! In his first Grand Prix in 1968 he put his Lotus on pole at Watkins Glen; in 1978 he put it on pole eight times and won the world championship. He drove Formula One from 1968 until 1982, and electrified Italy in 1982 at Monza by putting his Ferrari on pole having returned from retirement earlier that year to replace the injured Didier Pironi. He took third place, behind Patrick Tambay in second, the latter having replaced Gilles Villeneuve after Gilles's fatal accident at Zolder in May 1982. When Mario arrived at Milan airport, his plane was met by a large crowd of *tifosi* (the 'fevered ones') for whom he raised his arms in a V salute. He was received with acclamation fit for a king or a pope. He drove 128 Grands Prix and was placed in the top six thirty-eight times, on the front row twenty-four times and on pole eighteen times – this apart from winning Indy in 1969 and the CART title in 1984 at the age of forty-four. I had occasion to be upset with him once, at Jacarepagua, when somehow he got sideways at the start. The ensuing pile-up required a re-start – some time later. I had been hoping to spend the shortest possible time trapped in the medical car as I had Montezuma's Revenge . . .

I remember Mario hurting himself only once – in Zandvoort in August 1981 at the Dutch Grand Prix after an accident towards the end of the race when he hit the barrier. He bruised his leg and had some back pain, none of which seemed serious when he discussed his injuries in his usual laconic manner. At the next race in Italy he told me that X-rays in the USA had revealed a wedge-shaped fracture in one of his lumbar vertebrae, but said, 'It was OK,' and he raced nevertheless.

At Indianapolis in 2000 Mario was driving a Porsche in the Super Cup race although he had recently announced his retirement at the age of sixty! Unfortunately, I was so busy at

Indianapolis that I didn't see him, although I was following the two Porsche races for the first lap in the medical car – he's still fast enough to leave behind Alex Ribeiro and our five-litre AMG-converted Mercedes. If we had caught him he would have waved politely as he did when he was in trouble in the Formula One races and we passed him, which happened at Zandvoort in the S curves in 1979. His car was damaged in the first-lap shunt at the first corner, called Tarzan, when Clay Regazzoni and several other drivers went off. We had the president of the FIA, Jean-Marie Balestre, crammed into the rear seat of the Porsche 911, and Herbert Linge, driving, was sliding the car around for the fun of it.

Mario likes to call me 'Doc' and the way he says it always makes me feel proud.

NIKI LAUDA

I admire Niki Lauda immensely for his courage, intelligence, candour and wit. He is not an easy person to get to know but in the last five or six years, since Ayrton Senna's fatal accident, I have spent more time with him when he turns up at a Grand Prix. He, too, likes to frequent Karl-Heinz Zimmerman's motor-home.

I remember seeing him at Brands Hatch in the autumn of 1976 at a combined meeting of Formula One and Formula 5000. The edges of his skin graft had still not healed after his accident at Nürburgring in August that year. Despite his serious injuries, he had missed only the next two Grands Prix, in Austria and Holland, but drove at Monza less than six weeks after his crash and took fourth place. In 1974 and

1975, he put his Ferrari on pole eighteen times in twenty-nine events, and in 1976 was on the front row eight times in the first ten races, including the German race in which he crashed. Having won the world championship in 1975 he lost in 1976 by one point to James Hunt, even though he had missed two races and elected not to continue to drive in the appalling wet conditions in Japan. He regained the title in 1977, and at the end of the season left to join Brabham.

In 1979, much to everybody's consternation, he got out of his car on the Friday morning in Montreal and announced that he was fed up with driving around in circles. Bernie Ecclestone asked me what we should tell the press while Niki sorted himself out. I thought the old gastroenteritis ploy was a good cover but the truth was soon out. We didn't see much of him thereafter until 1982, when he returned to drive for McLaren in South Africa and led the infamous Grand Prix drivers' strike at a hotel near Kyalami. They spent the night watching each other restlessly to see who would break the strike first. He won the 1984 world championship after a clever drive at Estoril, beating team-mate Alain Prost by half a point as he drove quietly into second place. All in all, in 171 Grands Prix he was in the first six places seventy-three times, including twenty-five wins, twenty second places and nine thirds.

He is a safe road-car driver, and in 1979 drove me so courteously and smoothly to the circuit in Jarama that I was impressed. In the late 1990s a group of us, led by Niki, Karl-Heinz Zimmerman and Andrea Molinari – Niki's man in Havana – went to Cuba on a cigar outing, with Herbie Blash, Freddy Petersen, the distinguished journalist, Señor Faletti, a great photographer, and Bertl Wimmer, Niki's great friend.

Of course, we went Lauda Air, and had a fantastic time at the tobacco factories and plantations, with a fine party every evening. On the way back, via Cancun, the aeroplane broke down. Time spent in the bar waiting for it to be repaired resulted in one of the funniest sights I have ever seen: Karl-Heinz and Bertl Wimmer performing an Austrian oompa-pah waltz in the airport lounge, much to the enjoyment of our group and the consternation of other passengers.

His attitude to his 1976 accident epitomizes his cool, intellectual, cynically amused approach to life. He refers to the place where he had the accident as Barbecue corner. Not long after his accident somebody referred unwisely to his lost ear. Niki remarked, 'Very convenient to have no ear – you hear the telephone better when it's on the bone.'

On his fiftieth birthday, he and some friends went to the old circuit at Nürburgring to visit the site of the accident and have a few schnapps. While they were there, some German tourists turned up in the woods and, to their surprise, found Niki and his party. 'Niki Lauda, what are you doing here?' they cried.

'I'm looking for my ear,' Niki replied.

Niki has agreed to give the 2001 Motor Sport Fund Watkins Lecture at the autosport exhibition in Birmingham at the National Exhibition Centre. When I thanked him for agreeing to do it, he said, 'Wait till you get the bill for the Lear jet.'

NELSON PIQUET

Nelson is the naughtiest driver I have ever known and the most irreverent. In *Life at the Limit* I described how he used to tease Jean-Marie Balestre, President of the FIA, during the drivers' briefings by pouring a bottle of mineral water into Jean-Marie's blazer pocket, voting before the vote was proposed or using both arms to vote. However, he was at his most audacious one day when Jean-Marie was standing on the grid with his back to Nelson, who was in his race car. Suddenly a hand – Nelson's – appeared between his legs and grabbed the esteemed president you-know-where. Every time I see Nelson he attempts to rip open my flies, which is quite mild, I suppose.

In December 1999 when I was at the annual dinner of the French Fédération Société Automobile, appropriately enough at the Lido, on the Champs Élysées in Paris, Jean-Marie signalled me to his table – still very presidential in style. He was pleased with me because I had given an interview to *L'Équipe*, the French newspaper, on the evolution of safety measures and had paid due respect to him for the major contributions he had made. He thanked me graciously for my acknowledgement and we started to talk about Nelson Piquet and his mischief. Jean-Marie laughed and I told him I thought he had a soft spot for Nelson. He replied, 'You are right, I always love heem.' I haven't had the chance to tell Nelson this – the last time I saw him was at the Brazilian Grand Prix in 2000 when I needed to cross in front of him. He grabbed me from behind and pulled me on to his knees to give me a cuddle. At the age of forty-seven he still hasn't grown up!

He drove Formula One for fourteen years and was world champion three times in 1981, 1983 and 1987. He was brilliantly quick, and seemed utterly careless of safety. He drove in 204 races and was on pole twenty-four times and the front row in qualifying forty-four times. He won twenty-three Grands Prix but was in the top six places a hundred times – in approximately 50 per cent of all his races. He had severe accidents – the record shows thirty during races and plenty of others in practice sessions. But in Formula One he never hurt himself much. We were all very sad when he had his big accident at Indianapolis, injuring his legs severely and effectively ending his career.

DAMON HILL

I have to record how pleased I was when Damon won the world championship in 1996. He had been second in the two previous years and third in the points in his first full year in Formula One. Not only did he deserve his championship in 1996, he was right there at the top in those four consecutive years 1993–6 – a tribute to his driving ability. I was also pleased because he is such a gentleman, and I have never seen him put a foot wrong in his behaviour. In 1994 he was remarkably composed after the accident in Adelaide when he was in contention for the title and beaten by one point by Schumacher, who had collided with him and put them both off. Damon won three Grands Prix in 1993, six in 1994, and four in 1995, when he had a bad year but was second nevertheless in the world championship. In 1996 he won eight races, was second twice, with one fourth and one fifth place. Overall he won twenty-two Grands Prix, and was in the top six places fifty-six times in 115 Grands Prix – virtually 50 per cent of all his races. He was on the front row forty-seven times and had twenty pole positions. It is intriguing to see in Jacques Deschenaux's *Grand Prix Guide* Damon's statistics alongside his father's. It is notable that Damon notched up twenty-two wins in his 115 races and Graham fourteen in 176. Damon was especially skilled in wet conditions and put up some stunning performances in Brazil, Japan and Adelaide in adverse weather, and in 1998, in Spa, which he won in his last year in Grand Prix racing.

I gather he is a stunning performer on the guitar as well, although I have never witnessed this. I do know that he is a proficient golfer and he has helped me by playing regularly in the Grand Prix Drivers' Golf Charity Day for the British Brain and Spine Foundation. I did promise to teach him salmon fishing some years ago, but that was when he was driving Formula One and we never got time to try it together. Perhaps by now, in his 'retirement', he has taken up the sport but if he has not, my offer still holds. I hope he buys this book so that he can see it in writing.

GERHARD BERGER

Since he retired as a driver we have all missed Gerhard – he was light-hearted and always ready for a prank. He has been a dedicated member of the Advisory Expert Group and is immensely practical about safety matters.

He had a long career in Formula One: he competed in 210 Grands Prix and was in the first six places ninety-five times, with ten Grand Prix wins and thirty-two starts on the front row. He was a wonderfully loyal team-mate for Ayrton Senna at McLaren from 1990 to 1992. He drove for Ferrari for six years and won five Grands Prix for that team. His first Grand Prix win for Benetton in Mexico in 1986 was a wonderful surprise as he drove the whole race without a pit stop – much to everyone's consternation, as every other race car had had to go into the pit for new tyres.

I have picked Gerhard up with the medical car in practice when he's had big accidents, at Spa and Interlagos. According to the record he had twenty-five accidents during Grand Prix races, but he has always managed to avoid hurting himself too much, even at Imola, when his car burst into flames, and he got away with a brief concussion, some minor burns to his hand and a broken rib – which I might have caused while straddling him as he was coming round from his head injury and attempting to escape our ministrations. His worst injury was in a road-car accident in 1984 when he broke his neck; the fracture required a bone graft and metallic protection.

When he'd had a big shunt he used to like to lie down in the medical car for a while. Once at Monza, at the second chicane during the warm-up on Sunday, he had a serious one. By the time I arrived, he had been rescued and the spinal splint was in place. He was in the ambulance, heading for the medical centre, so I met him there. He told me that on the way in the ambulance, with the oxygen mask on his face, he had realized he couldn't breathe properly. Then he noticed that the oxygen tap had not been switched on so he reached up and turned it on himself. Laughing, he said, 'Get me out of here before I get damaged!'

As we were a bit worried that he might have stressed his

old neck injury, we sent him off to hospital for an X-ray. All was well and he climbed back into the car to race as if nothing had happened.

JUAN MANUEL FANGIO

I met Fangio only once, although in 1979 I saw him drive his Mercedes on a wet circuit at Donington when Bernie Ecclestone held a Formula One demonstration day to raise money to build and equip the new Gunnar Nilsson radiotherapy suite at the Charing Cross Hospital – where Gunnar had been treated for cancer. Gunnar was a promising young Swedish driver. His illness was diagnosed early in 1978. He died in October 1978 after only two seasons in Formula One, during which he won the Belgian Grand Prix at Zolder and was in the top six places in eight other Grands Prix. At the demonstration Fangio put on a spectacular display, with his Mercedes on opposite lock, drifting round the corners in his short-sleeved shirt and old soft-sided helmet.

I met him, at Bernie's request, at the circuit in Adelaide in 1988. Fangio had been giving a demonstration between the Formula One practice sessions on the Saturday when an unauthorized truck pulled on to the circuit. To avoid it Fangio spun his car rather than taking it from the rear. With great skill, he came to a stop alongside a tyre barrier without significantly damaging his car. But he had banged his elbow against the barrier and had a large swelling on his arm due to extreme bruising – it was a haematoma, a collection of blood. Bernie was anxious to know the great man had not fractured his elbow and summoned me. Fangio accepted my ministrations with mildly amused tolerance, and thanked me for my efforts.

Fangio drove in fifty-one Grands Prix of which he was on pole in twenty-eight and on the front row forty-eight times. He won twenty-four races, was second ten times, third once and fourth six times – placed forty-one times in all. He was world champion in 1951, and every year from 1954 to 1957 inclusive. He took his fifth title at the age of forty-six. He retired in 1958, winning pole position in his last but one race, fittingly in Argentina. No wonder Ayrton Senna worshipped him as a hero, and it was great to see them together in Adelaide. Had he survived, Ayrton might well have had the record number of championships.

JOHN SURTEES

I must not fail to pay my respects to John Surtees, who interpolated his World Championship in 1964 between those of Jim Clark in 1963 and 1965. I did not know him when he was racing, except to exchange greetings, but I have had the pleasure of driving round the odd circuit in recent years when he has been demonstrating his skill with the veteran F1 cars. The most recent occasion was at Suzuka this year when I gave him two laps before he drove the old Formula One Honda. He said quietly, 'I know its only a demonstration, but its as well to know what's round the corner even so.'

I first saw him race cars at Goodwood in 1962, when it appeared to me that he thought he was still on his motorbike as he tried to slip four wheels through impossibly narrow gaps when attempting to overtake. Later, I saw him at Sebring in

Above: Canada, 1997. Panis being tended by Canadian and FIA medical teams. My apologies for displaying his underpants.

Below: Belgium, 1998. Despite the carnage nobody was hurt. Only Barrichello, Panis, Rosset and Salo failed to re-start.

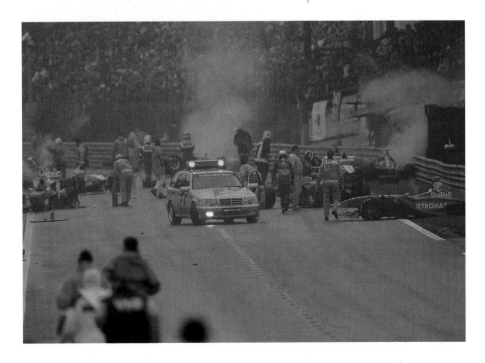

Opposite page: The Alchemist.

Above: Spa, 1966. Jackie Stewart's three friends in ecstasy. (*Jock McDonald*)

Right: Nurburgring, 1968. JYS wins by over four minutes!!

Left: Damon Hill, Champion 1996. I have <u>now</u> heard him play guitar at the Grand Prix Charity gala!

Below: Graham Hill, World Champion 1962, 1988. Graham always looked very determined and resolute in the car.

Above: Jim Clark, Champion 1963, 1965. Tragically lost at Hockenheim in 1968. A wonderful precise talent, and quiet, gentlemanly personality.

Right: Sir Stirling Moss. Every British young man's hero in the fifties and the sixties, including mine.

Left: Phil Hill, Champion 1961. Winning his first Grand Prix (1960) for Ferrari.

Below: Fangio, Le Mans. He was brilliant also at long distance racing.

Top right: Innes Ireland, Watkins Glen, 1961. Victorious; Innes is in characteristic pose.

Below right: Jack Brabham, thrice Champion. Laid back; Dean Delamont (striped tie) grinning.

The man in the white suit; earlier days, exotic cars.
The hat – new then – still going strong despite adverse comments.

1963, driving for Ferrari, in the twelve-hour race, for whom he drove prototypes as well as F1. His record is most impressive on both two wheels and four wheels. He was seven times Motorcycle World Champion winning sixty-eight races before he went full-time motor-car racing. In 1963, he joined Ferrari and was fourth in the World Championship behind Jim Clark, Graham Hill and Richie Ginther and in 1964 he won the championship. In 1966, he was second in the World Championship, (having left Ferrari early in the season), driving a Cooper Maserati for the rest of the year. He was placed forty times in 111 Grands Prix, and was on the front row twenty-two times in qualifying. In the sixties he raced in Can-Am, and won the first Can-Am Championship. He formed his own F1 team in 1970, and retired as a driver in 1971. He ranks, therefore, among the British World Championship drivers of the post-war era: Mike Hawthorn – whom I never met – Graham Hill, Jim Clark, Jackie Stewart, James Hunt, Nigel Mansell and Damon Hill. When will we see the next one, and who will it be – Coulthard or Button?

APPENDIX 1

THE WORK OF THE ADVISORY EXPERT GROUP

DEFINITION OF UNITS

Mass The mass of a body (M) is a measure of the amount of matter it contains.

Common units used are:
Kilogramme (kg) and pound (lb)
1kg = 2.20lb

Acceleration Acceleration is the increase in velocity in unit time or rate of change of velocity.

Common units used are:
Metres per second per second (m/s^2) and feet per second per second (ft/s^2)
$1m/s^2 = 3.28ft/s^2$

Gravity The acceleration due to gravity is 1g.
$1g = 9.81m/s^2 = 32.17ft/s^2$

Momentum Momentum is the mass (M) multiplied by velocity (V) = MV.

Units are Kg m/s or lb ft/s
1 Kg m/s = 7.23lb ft/s

Force Force is the mass multiplied by the acceleration.

1 Newton (N) is the force required to accelerate a mass of 1 kg one metre/sec^2
10,000 Newton (10KN) approximates to 2240lb force (1 ton)

Energy Energy is the sum of component energies. The sum of
Potential energy (mass $\times$ g $\times$ height above zero) = Mgh plus
Kinetic energy (mass $\times$ velocity squared divided by 2) = ½MV^2
The unit J is 1 Joule or 1 foot pound force
1 Joule equates with 0.738ft/lb force

Torque The unit of torque (Nm) is the Newton metre and is used in measuring bending force (as in the neck).

Radian The Rad is the angle at the centre of a circle the arc of which is equal in length to the radius.
1 Rad approximates to 57.3°
Rotational acceleration or deceleration is measured in Rads per second per second (rad/s^2).

1994–2000

In 1994 in addition to the fatal injuries to Roland Ratzenberger and Ayrton Senna at Imola, two drivers, J. J. Lehto and Jean Alesi, had fractures of the cervical spine (neck), fortunately without spinal cord injury, in accidents in private testing. Two drivers, Barrichello and Montermini, had head injuries with mild concussion and one driver, Wendlinger, had a severe head injury with coma in accidents in official practice. Shortly after these injuries Lamy received multiple injuries again in private testing. In all there had been eight serious accidents. Max Mosley, President of the Fédération Internationale Automobile, responded immediately, introducing changes to the cars to reduce speed and initiating an Advisory Expert Group to conduct research and development to effect greater safety. The committee consisted of Charlie Whiting, FIA Technical Chief, Peter Wright, FIA Adviser and ex-F1 race-car designer, Dr Harvey Postlethwaite, then Tyrrell designer, Roland Bruynseraede, F1 Race Director, Gerhard Berger and myself as Chairman. Immediately we commissioned the Motor Industries Research Association (MIRA) at Nuneaton to produce a study of the forces likely to be sustained by a driver in the cockpit (McLaren provided an F1 chassis) using high-G sled testing and Hybrid III instrumented dummies. The first results with frontal crash simulation at a velocity of 11.4 metre a second, a crash pulse of 23G (approximate speed 25 m.p.h.) are shown in Figure 1. The accepted limits for the threshold of head injury are shown on the left at 80G, over 3 milliseconds with a Head Injury Coefficient of 1,000. The Head Injury Criterion (HIC) is a complex calculation shown in Figure 2 which has been derived from road accident data correlated to head injury dependent on linear acceleration (or deceleration). The threshold limit for injury is believed to be 1,000 with a probable morality of 10 to 15 per cent, and as the figure mounts so does the threat to life and at HIC of 2,000 the chance of death exceeds 50 per cent.

Examining the results in the basic cockpit with two-inch shoulder harness, then standard, indicates the forward G when the head was thrown forward was 48G but the rebound G when the head was thrown back was 192, more than twice the injury threshold, and produced a HIC of 1,247. Work began to search for a foam that would provide energy absorption by deformation and to find the correct height to which the foam needed to be raised to be most effective. A Confor foam head and neck protection with a thickness of 75mm in the form of a U-shaped structure attached to the cockpit side and raised to reach the centre of gravity of the crash helmet/driver's head was found to be the best. The results achieved by this technique are shown on the extreme right of Figure 1 – forward G at 54, rearward G 83 and an HIC of 388.

Another device to restrain the head and neck was also tested – this called the HANS (head and neck protection system) – this was invented by Professor Hubbard of Michigan State University for high-speed motor-boat racing. It consisted of a solid yoke on the shoulders with extension piece behind and attached to the driver's helmet on each side at the rear. The results showed that restraining the forward movement of the dummy's head reduced the rebound rearward G to 130 and the HIC to 746 – not as efficient as the foam protection. This work was both painstaking and expensive for each test session cost several thousand pounds but Max Mosley had given us carte blanche intellectually and financially. He was as good as his word. The foam support was made compulsory at the beginning of 1996. Unfortunately too late to help in Hakkinen's accident in Adelaide in 1995 but early enough to protect Martin Brundle in his flying accident in the first race in 1996 in Melbourne. There was a great deal of reluctance on the part of the teams to accept the high cockpit sides and the larger cockpit necessary to accommodate the foam. My experiences about this are described elsewhere in the book. The device has prevented many serious injuries since 1996 and has also provided a basis for replicating accidents, as will be seen later.

Increasing the width of the shoulder harness and seatbelts to 3 inches also reduced forces in the chest from 65G in the basic cockpit to 43G, the tolerance limit being believed to be 60G over 3 milliseconds. The neck forces also fell in flexion to 44Nm from 65Nm and in extension from 17 to 15 – all being below the respective tolerances of 190 and 57, respectively.

In side impact (Figure 3) with a 35G pulse wave at 9.9 metres/second (approximate speed 22 m.p.h) the head and neck foam reduced the first lateral distortion forces from

79Nm to 13Nm with an injury threshold of 57Nm and the rebound force remained similar: 82Nm compared to 76Nm, well within the tolerance of 190Nm. In a subsequent test performed by MIRA when attempting to develop an air bag, a comparison was made with a frontal impact with the Confor foam protection alone and with a prototype air bag inflated on impact. Figure 4 shows with a crash pulse of 45g (approximate speed 34 m.p.h.) a 20-litre air bag reduced the peak G in the dummy head from 99G to 65G and the HIC from 975 to 509. Unfortunately the technology to develop an air bag to function in track conditions does not yet exist because of the speed of the accidents, the need to protect against multiple impacts and the necessity of avoiding accidental inflation.

Since 1996 there have been many serious incidents in F1 accidents and these are shown year by year in Figure 5, indicating in columns the driver, the circuit, the angle of impact (frontal, rear, lateral, oblique, inversion) and the effect on the driver. Those accidents marked with an asterisk have been replicated at the Transport Research Laboratory at Crowthorne by Andrew Mellor and Brian Chinn whose work and advice have been of immense value over recent years. In 1996, Jos Verstappen had a high-speed accident at Spa in which the contact with his helmet destroyed the Confor foam head rest. Analysis of the accident showed the forces to be 180G with an HIC of 1,980, the energy absorption of the crash helmet and the head protection foam were such that he was not unconscious but merely stunned and slightly unsteady on his feet when he got out of the car. Brain scanning subsequently that day showed no evidence of any injury. In 1995 in Hakkinen's accident, the G-forces were calculated as

208 with an HIC of 1,824 and the result was a fractured skull and unconsciousness, scanning showing evidence of injury. But the driver's helmet in this case contacted the cockpit side unprotected by foam as the head and neck protection had not been introduced.

In 1997 the FIA introduced compulsory accident data recorders to be fitted to all F1 cars. The results of the recordings in the accidents have been analysed by Peter Wright of the FIA and have provided much valuable physical data concerning the forces, impact speed and the evolution of the accident. The data has also been fundamental in accident replication since then.

Two further examples of high G-forces without significant head injury were experienced in 1999. In Schumacher's accident in Silverstone the G-forces were 122 with an HIC of 1,070. Frentzen later in the year in Canada was mildly concussed with a peak G of 124 and an HIC of 855 but the rotational forces in the brain were 5,278 radians per second per second against 4,021 in Schumacher's case. When the head rotates after impact, the semi-solid brain distorts in a circular fashion, and it has been recognized that the distortion can strain or shear the conducting nerve fibres within the brain stem and brain, and also bruise the surface of the brain against the irregular internal bony shapes of the compartments of the skull. The threshold of injury in terms of radians per second per second has been difficult to determine but recent work on the accident replication study shown in Figure 6 by Andrew Mellor and published at the meeting of the Society of Automotive Engineers in 2000 indicates a threshold of 5,000 radians per second per second, and the onset of serious injury at 1,000 radians per second per second, supporting previous assessment. Unfortunately brain injury forces cannot simply be linear acceleration or rotational acceleration but are a combination of both. Difficulty exists, therefore, in correlating neurological injury to simple physics. But clearly a combination of both linear and rotational forces produces contusion of the brain's surface and tearing of fibre systems, aside from rupture of vessels with consequential intracerebral and extracerebral bleeding. It should be noted in Figure 7 that the ten accidents which have been replicated are shown categorized by the protection that was available in the accident – namely crash helmet only or crash helmet with Confor foam head rest; more detailed neurological results are shown in descending order of severity. It is noted by Andrew Mellor that in Verstappen's accident there was a head-impact speed of 11 metres/second, the G-force was 180 and the HIC 1,980 (Figure 6, case 3). Without protection save for the crash helmet in case 9 a speed of head impact at 8.5 metres/second produced 295G and an HIC of 2,815. The driver was unconscious for some hours and had signs of neurological damage. In Andrew Mellor's paper he has published three graphs correlating the AIS (Abbreviated Injury Scale)* and injury caused with peak linear acceleration (Figure 8), peak rotational acceleration (Figure 9), and the relationship of peak rotational acceleration, peak linear acceleration and the AIS score (Figure 10).

* Abbreviated Injury Scale is a system designed to facilitate coding of injury potential with peak g values. Thus:

AIS 0 = < 50g   AIS 4 = 200–250g
AIS 1 = 50–100g   AIS 5 = 250–300g
AIS 2 = 100–150g   AIS 6 = > 300g
AIS 3 = 150–200g

Examination of the data revealed by this extremely important biophysical research suggests that the tolerance to injury for the drivers is higher than previously thought. Whether this is true for the general population is not known but certainly in these extremely fit, highly motivated young men they have gone 'Beyond the Limit'.

In the past three years there has been considerable development of the HANS system and Professor Hubbard, Hubert Gramling of Daimler Mercedes Benz and Peter Hodgman of McLaren have been modifying and testing at high speed the efficacy of the new HANS. Results show that wearing the HANS significantly reduces the forces exerted in the head and neck in direct frontal accidents and prevents the drivers' helmets from striking the steering wheel or, in the oblique accident, the cockpit side. A certain number of Formula One drivers have used the device in private testing. In fact, in CART racing some drivers have used the HANS to race, as has been the case in the German DTM series. In F1 cars wearing the device has been left voluntary and to the drivers' and teams' discretion. The experimental data gained by Hubert Gramling suggests that the reduction in forces is equal to that shown in air-bag tests that both MIRA and Hubert Gramling have performed. As a further aid to reduced injury from frontal impact, it has been mandatory since 1997 for the steering-wheel column to be collapsible and the energy absorption of the steering wheel, column and rack demonstrated by FIA impact test. For the year 2001 energy absorping foam is to be extended in the cockpit to protect the hips and legs.

Over the years 1994–2000 the FIA has continued to modify the cars, the barriers and the circuits to improve safety: the regulations imposed are shown in Appendix 2, which also lists the accidents and injuries in five-year blocks up to 1997. Since then the changes demanded each year are shown annually. Agreed in 2000 to be imposed this year are changes in the load testing to the head-protection rear-roll structure increased laterally from 12KN to 50KN, longitudinally from 45KN to 60KN and vertically from 60KN to 90KN. A side intrusion test for the monocoque has been increased to withstand a force of 150KN (15 tons). The existing side-impact test which demands energy absorption of 6,000 Joules. For 2001 to aid wheel retention double cables (breaking strain 5,000 Kg or 5 tons) tether each wheel to the chassis – previously only one cable to each wheel had been demanded.

Fortunately, in the year 2000, though it brought spectacular accidents, there were no significant injuries at all.

Over the years, the composition of the Advisory Expert Group has changed, as has its title. We tragically lost Dr Harvey Postlethwaite who died unexpectedly and whose place has been taken by John Barnard. Gerhard Berger, after his appointment to the BMW Williams Team, was unable to attend regularly and Michael Schumacher is now the Formula One driver in the group. Herbie Blash, the Assistant Race Director, has joined the committee. We frequently have the advice of Hubert Gramling from Daimler Mercedes Benz and Andrew Mellor from the Transport Research Laboratory. In the reorganization of the committee structure of the FIA which occurred in 1999 the Advisory Expert Group was reconstituted as the Research Commission, of which I remain the President.

FIGURE 1: HYGE TEST

HEAD (Crash Pulse 23G, velocity 11.4 metres/second)			
LIMIT	**BASELINE** (1964 Cockpit)	**HANS** (1964 Cockpit)	**PRESENT** (75mm Confor foam)
80g (3 milliseconds)	48F, 192B	54F, 130B	54F, 83B
HIC (1,000)	1247	746	388

FIGURE 2: HEAD INJURY CRITERION (HIC)

$$\left(\frac{1}{t^1-t^2} \int_{t^1}^{t^2} a.d\,t \right)^{2.5} \left(t^1-t^2 \right) < 1000$$

HIC> 1000 – 15% life threatening
HIC> 1400 – 50% fractured skull
HIC> 2000 – 50% life threatening head injury

Symbols t^1 and t^2 are the estimated times of the beginning and ending of the crash pulse which provide the highest HIC number calculable.

Symbol a is the integral of acceleration during the crash pulse with respect to time.

FIGURE 3: HYGE TEST

SIDE IMPACT (Crash pulse 35G, velocity 9.9 metres/second)

	LIMIT	BASE (1994 Cockpit)	PRESENT (Confor Foam 75mm)
Head 80g		66	86
HIC 1000		466	659
Neck			
1st Distortion 57Nm		79	13
Rebound 190Nm		76	82

FIGURE 4: HYGE TEST

HEAD AND NECK PROTECTION (Crash Pulse 45G, 55 $^{km}/_{hr}$)		
FRONTAL CRASH	PRESENT COCKPIT (Cockpit Confor foam 75mm)	PRESENT COCKPIT WITH AIR BAG 52 (20 Litre)
LIMITS (HEAD)		
Peak G 80	99	65
At 3MS 80		
HIC 1000	975	509

FIGURE 5: SERIOUS INCIDENTS

YEAR	NAME	PLACE	TYPE OF ACCIDENT	NEUROLOGICAL RESULT
1996	Verstappen*	Spa	Frontal	Minor
	Herbert	Spa	Frontal	Nil
	Coulthard	Silverstone (testing)	Oblique	Nil
1997	Berger	Montreal	Lateral	Nil
	Alesi	Montreal	Lateral	Nil
	Barrichello	Jerez	Lateral	Nil
1998	Salo	Montreal	Frontal	Nil
	Salo*	Spa	Frontal	Nil
	Frentzen	Magny Cours (testing)	Frontal	Nil
	Villeneuve	Spa	Rear Impact	Nil
	Rosset	Zeltweg	Lateral	Nil
		Hockenheim	Lateral	Nil
1999	Zonta	Interlagos	Frontal	Nil
	Frentzen*	Montreal	Oblique	Minor
	Schumacher*	Silverstone	Frontal	Nil
	Diniz	Nürburgring	Inversion	Nil
	Villeneuve	Spa	Rear Impact	Nil

* Accident replication performed

FIGURE 6: REPLICATION OF MOTOR SPORTS ACCIDENTS (FIA-TRL)

	Impact Surface	Impact Velocity $^m/_s$		Acceleration			AIS	Injury
		Norm	Tang	g	HIC	rad/s²		
Accident 1*	Cockpit	3	10	208	1824	6000	4	Serious
Accident 2*	Retaining wall	13	44	850	24000	37000	6	Fatal
Accident 3	Headrest	11	2	180	1980	5700	1	Slight
Accident 4*	Rollcage	15	13	1000	26000	14500	5	Serious
Accident 5*	Safety barrier	22	0	360	5000	11100	4	Serious
Accident 6*	Retaining wall	12	27	500	8500	34000	6	Fatal
Accident 7	Headrest	6	1.6	126	578	2147	0	Nil
Accident 8	Headrest	9	0	122	1070	4021	0	Nil
Accident 9*	Cockpit	8.5	0	295	2815	13016	4	Serious
Accident 10	Headrest	6.7	0	124	855	5276	0	Slight

* No Confor foam protection

Reproduced courtesy of Andrew Mellor, Transport Research Laboratory, Crowthorne, Berkshire

FIGURE 7: CORRELATION

PROTECTION		G FORCE >80.3ms	HIC 1,000	ROT^N 10,000	RESULT
Crash Helmet Only					
F3000	Wall	850	24,000	37,000	Fatal
F1	Wall	500	8,500	34,000	Other fatal injuries sustained
Sports Car 2 Impacts	Rollcage	1,000	26,000	14,500	Vegetative State
F1	Safety barrier	360	5,000	34,000	Decerebrate (recovery)
F3	Cockpit	295	2,815	13,016	Coma (recovery)
F1 2 Impacts	Cockpit	70 208	100 1,824	6,000	Coma (recovery)
Confor Foam Headrest					
F1 only	Headrest	180	1,980	5,700	Minor
F1	Headrest	126	578	2,147	Nil
F1	Headrest	122	1,070	4,021	Nil
F1	Headrest	124	855	5,276	Minor
Awaiting Analysis with ADR Data					
9 other impacts with destruction of headrest without head/neck injury.					

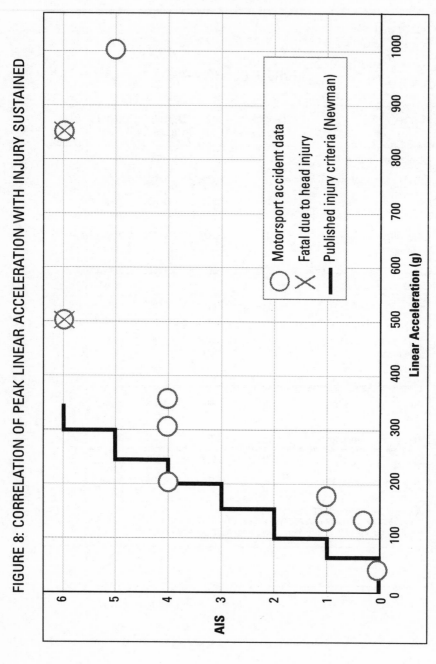

FIGURE 8: CORRELATION OF PEAK LINEAR ACCELERATION WITH INJURY SUSTAINED

Reproduced courtesy of Andrew Mellor, Transport Research Laboratory, Crowthorne, Berkshire

FIGURE 9: CORRELATION OF PEAK ROTATIONAL ACCELERATION WITH INJURY SUSTAINED

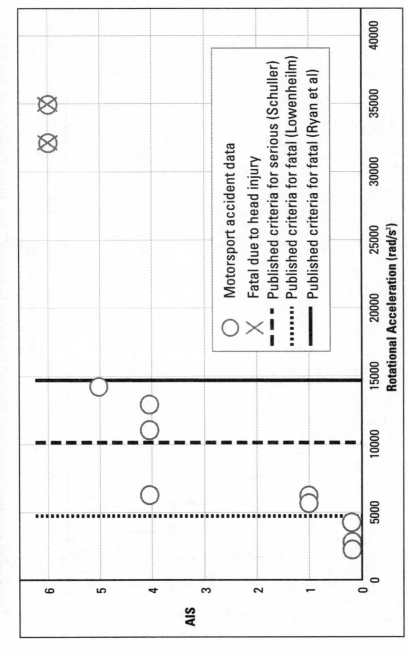

Reproduced courtesy of Andrew Mellor, Transport Research Laboratory, Crowthorne, Berkshire

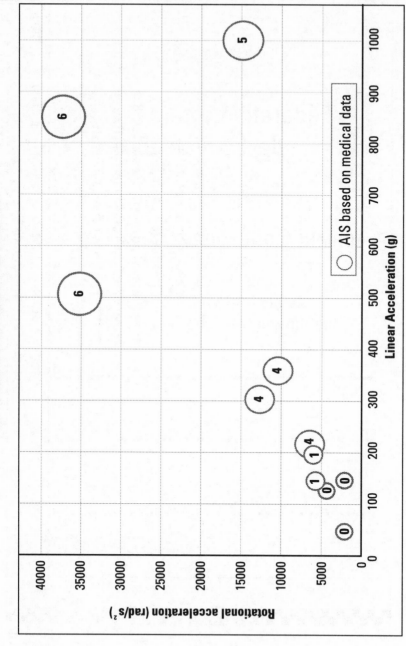

FIGURE 10: CORRELATION OF PEAK ROTATIONAL ACCELERATION, PEAK LINEAR ACCELERATION AND AIS

Reproduced courtesy of Andrew Mellor, Transport Research Laboratory, Crowthorne, Berkshire

APPENDIX 2

Fédération Internationale de L'Automobile

FORMULA ONE WORLD CHAMPIONSHIP

Safety in Grand Prix racing in
the thirty-seven years from 1963–1999

A STUDY BY THE CIRCUITS AND SAFETY DEPARTMENT

This document indicates the development of Formula One racing and the corresponding increase in the number of race incidents, over the period 1963–99, in which unprecedented advances in the application of technology and aerodynamics to the cars produced remarkable potential for increasing performance. It shows for each period considered the continuous action taken by the FIA and the Formula One Teams in developing and applying measures progressively to contain the consequences of accidents, latterly achieving levels of risk which are minimal for participants and negligible for spectators.

Although the example of Formula One only is considered here, the increases in both racing activity and safety have been reflected in every branch of motor sport under the control of the FIA.

FIA FORMULA ONE WORLD CHAMPIONSHIP

Safety in Grand Prix racing, 1963–1999

	THE INTRODUCTION OF SAFETY REGULATIONS BY THE FIA				
PERIOD	ACCIDENTS	CARS	CIRCUITS	DRIVERS	ORGANIZATION
1963–1967	GP races: **50** Estimated racing kms: **256,000** Accidents in races: **47** Injuries, drivers: **2** Fatalities, drivers: **3** Fatalities, officials: **0** Fatalities, spectators: **0**	**1963–65:** Pump fuel only. Automatic starter; rollbar; double braking system; vrilles for seat-belt anchorages, fire protection, fuel tanks, fillers and breathers.	FIA begins to organize circuit safety inspections (previously done by national authorities).	Protective helmet and overalls obligatory.	**1963:** Flag signalling code.
1968–1972	GP races: **59** Estimated racing kms: **227,000** Accidents in races: **88** Injuries, drivers: **3** Fatalities, drivers: **4** Fatalities, officials: **0** Fatalities, spectators: **0**	**1968:** Electrical circuit breaker; reverse gear; cockpit designed for easy evacuation; oil catch tank; rollbar 5cm above driver's helmet. **1969:** Two extinguisher systems; parts with aerodynamic influence must be immobile, fixed to sprung	**1970:** Considerations on circuit design published: track verges minimum 3m; double guardrails; spectators at least 3m behind fencing; barrier between pit lane and track; track width, surface and gradient change regulations; straw bales	**1968:** Recommendations on seat harnesses, fire-resistant clothing, shatterproof visors. **1971:** Max. 5 seconds for driver evacuation from cockpit. **1972:** 6-point harness. Drivers' Code of Conduct published.	**1971:** personnel, equipment and duties specified in race supervision marshalling, signals.

Continued

THE INTRODUCTION OF SAFETY REGULATIONS BY THE FIA

PERIOD	ACCIDENTS	CARS	CIRCUITS	DRIVERS	ORGANIZATION
1968–1972 continued		parts of car only; maximum bodywork height & width limits. **1970:** Safety bladder fuel tanks. **1972:** Safety foam in fuel tanks; no magnesium sheet less than 3mm thick; 15W red rear light; headrest; minimum cockpit dimensions; combined electrical cut-off/extinguisher external handle; FIA/spec/FT3 fuel tank.	banned; mandatory FIA inspections. **1972:** Circuit Safety Criteria published; debris fence specifications.	Drivers' Code of Conduct published. **1973:** International medical card & examination for all drivers.	
1973–1977	GP races: **77** Estimated racing kms: **446,000** Accidents in races: **250** Injuries, drivers: **5** Fatalities, drivers: **5** Fatalities, officials: **1** Fatalities, spectators: **6** **N.B.:** the spectators killed had all penetrated prohibited areas.	**1973:** Crushable structure round fuel tank; no chrome plating of suspension parts. **1974:** Self-seal breakaway fuel coupling. **1976:** 'Safety structures' around dashboard and pedals. **1977:** Pedal-box protection defined.	**1973:** Catch fences; rescue equipment; starting-grid dimensions. **1974:** Catch fences + sand. **1975:** Marshal posts; service roads. **1977:** Gravel arrester beds defined.	**1975:** FIA standard for fire resistant clothing. **1977:** Helmets must be to FIA-approved standards.	**1973:** Fire service regs. **1975:** Medical service; resuscitation centre; obligatory rescue exercise. **1974:** 2 × 2 staggered starting grid with 12m length per car.

THE INTRODUCTION OF SAFETY REGULATIONS BY THE FIA

PERIOD	ACCIDENTS	CARS	CIRCUITS	DRIVERS	ORGANIZATION
1978–1982	GP races: **76** Estimated racing kms: **399,000** Accidents in races: **283** Injuries, drivers: **3** Fatalities, drivers: **3** Fatalities, officials: **1** Fatalities, spectators: **0**	**1978:** Bulkhead behind driver and front rollbar defined. **1979:** Bigger cockpit opening; 2 mirrors; improved extinguisher system. **1981:** Reinforced 'survival cell' introduced and extended in front of driver's feet.	**1980:** Obligatory permanent medical centre. **1981:** Tyre barriers; pit-lane minimum width 10m.	**1978:** Licence qualification requirements. **1979:** Life support system (medical air) obligatory.	**1978:** Grid 14m per car. **1979:** FIA-appointed permanent race starters. **1980:** FIA approval of medical service obligatory; fast rescue car regulations. **1981:** Grid 1×1×1.
1983–1987	GP races: **79** Estimated racing kms: **428,000** Accidents in races: **218** Injuries, drivers: **2** Fatalities, drivers: **0** Fatalities, officials: **1** Fatalities, spectators: **0**	**1983:** Flat bottom obligatory; skirts banned; red light increased to 21W. **1984:** Refuelling in races banned; fuel tank in centre of car. **1985:** Frontal crash test.	**1984:** Concrete wall may replace guardrails. **1985:** Catch fences banned. **1987:** Criteria for temporary circuits.	**1984:** F1 'Super licence' required.	**1986:** Permanent FIA medical service inspector. Medical helicopter obligatory. **1987:** Grid 16m per car.
1988–1992	GP races: **80** Estimated racing kms: **478,000** Accidents in races: **305** Injuries, drivers: **1** Fatalities, drivers: **0** Fatalities, officials: **0** Fatalities, spectators: **0**	**1988:** Driver's feet behind front wheel axis; static crash test of survival cell and fuel tank. **1990:** Larger mirrors; quickly detachable steering-wheel. **1991:** FIA tested seat-belts; FT5 fuel tanks; rollbar test;	**1989:** Trackside barrier min. height 1m; pit wall min. 1.35m. **1992:** Kerbs lowered; pit lane min. width 12m; pit entry chicane obligatory.	**1989:** Dope testing on IOC model introduced.	**1988:** Permanent FIA race director. **1990:** Driver extrication exercise obligatory. **1992:** Safety car introduced. **1993:** Pit-lane speed limited to 50k.p.h. in practices.

Continued

THE INTRODUCTION OF SAFETY REGULATIONS BY THE FIA

PERIOD	ACCIDENTS	CARS	CIRCUITS	DRIVERS	ORGANIZATION
1988–1992 continued		dynamic test of survival cell. **1992:** More severe impact tests: water-filled fuel tank fitted to test strength of seat back bulkhead and 75kg dummy fitted with maximum deceleration figure for the torso (also verifies harness anchorage strength).			
1993–1997	GP races: **82** Estimated racing kms: **450,000** Accidents in races: **382** Injuries, drivers: **11** Fatalities, drivers: **2** Fatalities, officials: **0** Fatalities, spectators: **0**	**1993:** Headrest area increased (from 80cm² to 400cm²). Front overhang reduced (100cm to 90cm). Rear wing height above ground reduced (100cm to 95cm). Distance of front wing endplates above the flat bottom increased (25mm to 40mm). Complete wheel width reduced (18" to 15"). Fuel regulations restricted to permit only fuels of a kind used by the general public.	**1994:** Pits spectator gallery fire shield obligatory. Identification of 27 'very high risk' corners by computer analysis: 15 removed from list by 1994 performance reductions. Tyre wall deceleration tests, analysed relative to human tolerance levels, produce a standard by which to judge new barriers. Use of conveyor belting in front of tyre walls recommended. **1995:** Smooth raised kerbs	**1993–on:** Severe end-of-race crowd control measures imposed. **1994:** Approved helmet standards reduced to 3 most stringent (Sell/BSI/SFI). Ear-phones banned; weight 1800g max. Checktests made on clothing and helmets in use. **1995:** 3-inch wide seat harness shoulder straps obligatory. Drivers' Super licence criteria more stringent.	**1994:** Pit-lane speed limited to 80k.p.h. in practice, 120 k.p.h. in the race. Fire-protective clothing for all refuelling crews. Burns treatment material in each pit obligatory. Pit-lane access new restrictions. Creation of the Advisory Expert Group, to apply new technology to safety. **1995:** Minimum safety services recommended for private testing. Clarification of blue, yellow and white

Continued

THE INTRODUCTION OF SAFETY REGULATIONS BY THE FIA

PERIOD	ACCIDENTS	CARS	CIRCUITS	DRIVERS	ORGANIZATION
1993–1997 continued		**1994:** Wheels must be made from an homogeneous metallic material. More stringent fire extinguisher regulations. Minimum thickness of the headrest 75mm (no minimum previously). Cockpit area side load test increased (from 2000daN to 3000daN). Driver aids (traction control, anti-lock and power brakes, automatic gears) banned. Four wheel steering no longer permitted. Downforce reduced: smaller front wing end-plates, shorter diffuser, deflector panels restricted. Pump fuel compulsory. 10mm skid block under reference plane. **1995:** Engine capacity reduced: 3.5 to 3.0 litres. Chassis must extend at least 30cm in front of	recommended. Gravel bed waves and furrows deleted. First pit wall debris shields installed. **1996:** Corners classified 'high risk' reduced to 2 through circuit safety improvements and track modifications. Temporary circuit wall and debris fence specification guidelines. FIA test requirement for 'thin' energy absorbing barriers. **1997:** FIA circuit approval required for testing. Kerb types and heights standardized after year of investigation. Bolted tyre wall construction obligatory. Analysis of the performance of safety measures with data recorded on the cars' ADRs.	**1996:** Safety-belt release lever must point downwards. **1997:** FIA supervision of conditions for private testing.	flag rules. FIA Doctor given Technical Assistant. **1996:** Standardization of FIA medical and safety-cars. Improved safety car procedure. Fire exercises with teams. Transformation of starting lights and procedure. **1997:** FIA approval for all Chief Medical Officers and medical centres. Revised accident intervention plan. Safety car: more powerful; may be used for wet race starts; permanent.

Continued

THE INTRODUCTION OF SAFETY REGULATIONS BY THE FIA

PERIOD	ACCIDENTS	CARS	CIRCUITS	DRIVERS	ORGANIZATION
1993–1997 continued		driver's feet (previously 15cm). Frontal impact test speed increased (from 11 to 12m/s). All deformation after the test must be confined to the nose box. Load in the nose push-off test increased (by 33% from 3000daN to 4000daN). Survival cell side impact test introduced. Obligatory automatic neutral selection when the engine stops. Introduction of a stepped flat bottom. Reduce front wing endplate heights (to between 5cm and 25cm above flat bottom) and length (must not extend further back than 35cm in front of the front wheel axis). No bodywork (wings) above rear wheels. Rear wing max. height reduced by 10cm.			

THE INTRODUCTION OF SAFETY REGULATIONS BY THE FIA

PERIOD	ACCIDENTS	CARS	CIRCUITS	DRIVERS	ORGANIZATION
1993–1997 continued		**1996:** Front wing endplates min. 10mm thick to prevent tyre damage to cars in front. Data storage unit to be within survival cell. Higher cockpit sides. 75mm side headrests compulsory. Static load test both sides of cockpit rim. Size of rear 'winglets' reduced. **1997:** FIA Accident Data Recorder (ADR) obligatory on all cars. Energy absorbing structure on gear-box imposed, with rear impact test. Energy absorption of steering wheel, column and rack must be shown by impact test. Bodywork rules to exclude rear 'winglets' and midship wings. Suspension must be designed to prevent contact of a front wheel with the driver's head in an			

Continued

THE INTRODUCTION OF SAFETY REGULATIONS BY THE FIA

PERIOD	ACCIDENTS	CARS	CIRCUITS	DRIVERS	ORGANIZATION
1993–1997 continued		accident and to provide 120° articulation of the forward lower arms, front and rear, to help retain the wheels.			
1998	GP races: **16** Estimated racing kms: **83,000** Accidents in races: **60** Injuries, drivers: **1** Fatalities, drivers: **0** Fatalities, officials: **0** Fatalities, spectators: **0**	Overall width reduced from 2m to 1.8m; grooved tyres made obligatory, to reduce cornering speeds. Single fuel bladder mandatory. Refuelling connector must be covered. Cockpit dimensions increased; side headrests extended to steering wheel. Mirror size increased, 5cm × 10cm to 5 × 12. Front roll hoop test introduced; survival cell dimensions forward of dash increased; side impact test speed increased (nearly 100% more energy), site moved forward 200mm.	High performance tyre barrier test specification established. Pit lane should be straight 100m before pits. Increased use of full light sets to supplement flag signals.	Two shoulder strap anchorages recommended. Driver must be able to exit and replace steering wheel, in 10 seconds.	

195

Continued

THE INTRODUCTION OF SAFETY REGULATIONS BY THE FIA

PERIOD	ACCIDENTS	CARS	CIRCUITS	DRIVERS	ORGANIZATION
1999	GP races: **17** Estimated racing kms: **88,000** Accidents in races: **60** Injuries, drivers: **2** Fatalities, drivers: **0** Fatalities, officials: **0** Fatalities, spectators: **0**	Engine oil breathers to vent into the engine air intake. A cable must tether each wheel to the chassis to prevent it flying off or contacting the driver's head, in case of accident. A seat which can be extracted with the driver in it in case of injury is mandatory.* Use of beryllium alloys in the chassis is prohibited. Frontal impact test: speed and maximum permitted average deceleration increased (from 12 to 13m/s and 25 to 40g). Distance of the driver's helmet below a line between the roll hoops increased (from 50 to 70mm). Rear and lateral headrests to be one-piece, with standard quick-release	Pit wall debris fences becoming generalized. Recommended to widen the signalling platform by 50cm, for circulation (obligatory for new circuits). Asphalt used on some run-off locations.	Highly visible gloves recommended for signalling startline problems. 'Marshal Information Display' lights system to be fitted in cockpit. Seat belts must comply with FIA Standard 8853–98.	At least 4 medical intervention cars + FIA Doctor car obligatory. Pit lane exit control by red and green lights and blue warning flag, practice and race

* Dr. J. J. Isserman has been responsible for the training of the extrication teams worldwide in the use of the extractable seat.

Continued

THE INTRODUCTION OF SAFETY REGULATIONS BY THE FIA

PERIOD	ACCIDENTS	CARS	CIRCUITS	DRIVERS	ORGANIZATION
1999 continued		method. Asymmetric braking prohibited. The FIA Accident Data Recorder must also be in operation in private testing.			
2000	GP races: **17** Estimated racing kms: **92,000** Accidents in races: **62** Injuries, drivers: **0** Fatalities, drivers: **0** Fatalities, officials: **1** Fatalities, spectators: **0**	Cable restraint for each wheel, breaking strain 50KN, minimum diameter of 8mm. Survival cell side tests of conforming pads to be applied to the outer surface of the survival cell must confirm no structural failure with transverse horizontal loads of 25KN and 30KN.			

NOTE: 'Estimated kms' refers to racing only; practice sessions at events would increase this by up to 150%.

APPENDIX 3

Formula One Injury Statistics
1978–2000

BURNS

When I first started working for Bernie Ecclestone in 1978 the worst fears about fire in F1 still prevailed. The accident to Niki Lauda in 1976 when he nearly lost his life was fresh in our minds and I still vividly remember the huge plume of black smoke at Brands Hatch in 1971 from the fire in which Jo Siffert died.

However, experience in the last twenty-three years has shown that the regulations concerning fuel tanks, fuel coupling and fuel tank protection have reduced the risks considerably. As shown in Table 1 there have been no serious burns despite fire in the accidents of Peterson (1978), Paletti (1982), Ghinzani (1985) and Berger (1989) – the last due in particular to rapid intervention by the fire fighting service of the CEA (Constructions Estintori Automatica). The most spectacular incident was a pit-lane fire at Hockenheim in 1994 during refuelling when Verstappen and six pit crew received minor burns. Overall an immense improvement occured in burns hazard. In the millennium year there were no incidents.

UPPER LIMB INJURY

There have been surprisingly few injuries to the upper limbs, as is indicated in Table 2. Rupert Keegan sustained a compound fracture of the metacarpals (hand bones) in Zandvoort in 1978 and Gianni Morbidelli fractures of the radius and ulna (forearm bones) in testing at Magny Cours – both injuries requiring surgical treatment. There were no injuries in the 2000 season.

LOWER LIMB INJURY (TABLE 3)

In the early years leg, ankle and foot fractures were common until the frontal crash test was introduced at the insistence of the FIA President Jean-Marie Balestre. This measure, together with the extensions of the survival cell beyond the drivers' feet in 1981 after Regazzoni's accident in Long Beach in 1980, has reduced the risk considerably. In 1988 the regulation demanding the drivers' feet to be behind the front wheel axis has further reduced the likelihood of injury. In the recent accidents of Panis in 1997 and Schumacher in 1999 there was a failure of the chassis in each case. In 2000 there was only bruising of the knees in Johnny Herbert's crash in the Malaysian Grand Prix.

SPINAL INJURIES (TABLE 4)

Though there have been few with serious consequences, the results in these cases are tragic – in particular cervical injury to Philippe Strieff resulting in quadriplegia, and thoracic injury causing paraplegia for Clay Regazzoni. In the two fatal cases, the cervical injury was the cause of death and in Ratzenberger's accident the spinal injury was associated with a fatal head injury.

The lumbar injury sustained has been in the two cases compression (crush) fracture of the vertebral body without any neurological consequences.

There was no spinal injury in the 2000 season.

HEAD INJURY (TABLE 5)

Head injury has been the most serious threat to life and health in F1 racing, though it has been fortunate that in the seven serious head injuries four drivers survived and recovered, namely: Brambilla, Donnelly, Wendlinger and Hakkinen. Minor head injury with concussion was common until 1996. The effect of the introduction of the head and neck protection is demonstrated.

There were no head injury in the year 2000.

MORTALITY IN F1 AND IN ROAD ACCIDENTS

The distribution over the years is shown in Table 6. In the twenty-three years 1978–2000 we have lost seven drivers, which compares favourably with other sports. For example, in the UK in a similar twenty-five year period there were fourteen fatal injuries in rugby football and in the last eighteen months in cross-country eventing there have been nine deaths worldwide. In rugby football spinal injuries have also been prominent, approximately ten cases each year with paralysis due to spinal cord injury.

Outside sport in the European Union about 25,000 deaths per year occur in car accidents and the overall mortality on the roads is approximately 50,000. In the UK in 1996 there were 3,600 road deaths, and 3,000 deaths in accidents in the home.

Collected figures by the RAC (Table 7) show that between 1961 and 1996 – thirty-six years including circuit, karting, drag, sprint/hill and rally racing – there were 130 deaths, averaging 3.61 per year.

ACCIDENT STATISTICS

Analysis by Peter Wright of accident statistics from 1963–1992 in five-year tranches are shown graphically in Tables 8 and 9. The progressive reduction in serious injury or death rate per number of accidents is dramatic. Whereas in the period 1963–7 there was one death or serious injury per ten accidents, in the period 1987–92 the injury rate was one per 300 accidents.

In 1994 there was a spate of accidents and injuries with two deaths leading to the new measures already described. Since 1996, when the head and neck protection was introduced, there have been no significant head or neck injuries and the only injuries of note were to the legs of Panis and Schumacher when on each occasion the chassis failed.

This should, however, not lead to a sense of complacency, for the unexpected can always occur.

TABLE 1

	BURNS		
	Severe	Moderate	Minor
1978–84 (105 G.P.)	0	1	1
1985–91 (112 G.P.)	0	0	1
1992–2000 (145 G.P.)	0	0	1 +6 crew in pit lane fire

TABLE 2

ARM/HAND FRACTURES

	Severe	Minor
1978–84	1 metacarpal	0
1985–91	0	0
1992–2000	1 Radius and ulna	0

TABLE 3

LEG AND FOOT FRACTURES

	Severe	Minor
1978–84	10	2
FRONTAL CHASSIS CRASH TEST INTRODUCED 1985		
1985–91	3	1
1992–2000	3	1

TABLE 4: SPINAL FRACTURE

	1978–84	1985–91	1992–9
CERVICAL			
Severe	1 (FATAL)	1 (QUADRIPLEGIA)	0
Serious (without neurological damage)	0	0	3
THORACIC			
Severe	1 (PARAPLEGIA)	0	1 with fatal head Injury
LUMBAR			
Severe	0	0	0
Moderate (without neurological damage)	2	0	0

TABLE 5: HEAD INJURY

	SEVERE or FATAL	MINOR (Concussion)
1978–84	2	2
1985–91	1	6
1992–5	4	4
1996 Introduction of High Cockpit Sides with Foam Head and Neck Protection		
1996	0	1
1997	0	0
1998	0	0
1999	0	1
2000	0	0

TABLE 6

MORTALITY

	Race	Practice	Testing
1978–82	2	1	1
1983–7	0	0	1
1988–92	0	0	0
1993–7	1	1	0
1998	0	0	0
1999	0	0	0
2000	0	0	0
367 races	3	2	2

211

TABLE 7: SUMMARY BY YEAR OF FATALITIES BY DISCIPLINE

		RACE		SPEED		RALLY	GRAND TOTAL
		Car	Kart	Drag	Sprint/Hill		
	1961	3			1		4
	1962	3			2		5
	1963	4			2		6
	1964	5			2	1	8
	1965	4			1		5
	1966	2					2
	1967	1	1		1		3
	1968	6					6
	1969	4	1				5
	1970	4	2		1	1	8
	1971	6	1			1	8
	1972	2					2
	1973	2					2
	1974	7	1				8
	1975						0
	1976			1			1
	1977	1				1	2
	1978		1			1	2
	1979		1	2		2	5
	1980	3		1			4
	1981	2	2			1	5
1961–1986	1982				1		1
26 years	1984		1	1		1	3
64 deaths	1985	3				1	4
(car racing)	1986	1		1			2
	Subtotal	64	12	6	11	11	104

Reproduced courtesy of the RAC

Continued

Continued

		RACE		SPEED		RALLY	GRAND TOTAL
		Car	Kart	Drag	Sprint/ Hill		
	1987	3	1	1			5
	1988					1	1
	1989					2	2
	1990	1	1		1		3
1987–1996	1991	3					3
10 years	1992	3					3
11 deaths	1993		2		2	1	5
(car racing)	1994	1	1			1	3
	1995				1		1
	1996						0
	Subtotal	11	5	1	4	5	26
36 years	Total (36)	75	17	7	15	16	130
75 deaths	Av. yr	2.08	0.47	0.190	0.42	0.44	3.61
2.08 per Yr	Av. 10 yr	1.10	0.60	0.100	0.40	0.60	2.80
Per 000 competitors							
	'000s	68.4	47.8	38		121.1	276.3
	Av. 10 yr	0.18	0.10	0.13		0.04	0.08

All forms of racing in 36 years: 130 deaths = 3.6 per year

213

TABLE 8: F1 ACCIDENT STATISTICS

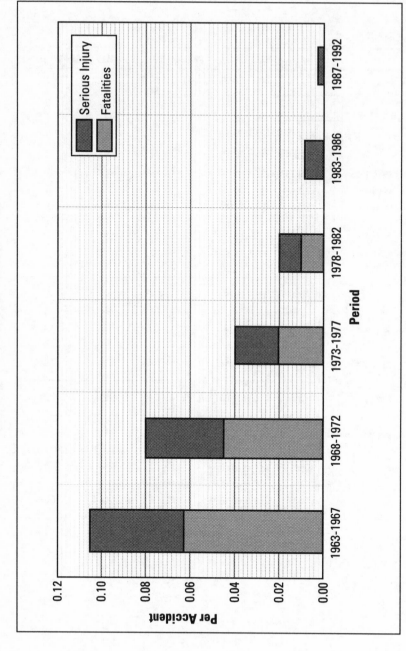

Reproduced courtesy of the FIA

TABLE 9: ACCIDENT STATISTICS

	FATAL/SERIOUS INJURIES
Early 1960s (1963–7)	1 per 10 accidents
Late 1960s (1968–72)	1 per 12 accidents
Early 1970s (1973–7)	1 per 25 accidents
Late 1970s (1978–82)	1 per 50 accidents
Early 1980s (1983–7)	1 per 100 accidents
Late 1980s (1988–92)	1 per 300 accidents

INDEX

ILLUSTRATION CREDITS

1. Brazil, 2000. Eddie Irvine. (LAT)
2. Australia, 2000. Michael Schumacher. (Allsport)
3. Austria, 2000. The medical car team.
4. Nürburgring, Germany, 1998. Herman 'the German'.
5. Monaco, 2000. Traffic jam. (LAT)
6. Austria, 2000. First corner accident (LAT)
7. Austria, 2000. Hakkinen, Coulthard, and Barrichello. (Allsport)
8. Indianapolis, 2000. Circuit. (LAT)
9. Johnny Herbert and Eddie Irvine.(Allsport)
10. Jenson Button. (Allsport)
11. Germany 2000. Michael Schumacher and Giancarlo Fisichella. (LAT)
12. Nürburgring, Germany, 1999. (Sutton Images)
13. Nürburgring, Germany, 1999. (Sutton Images)
14. Nürburgring, Germany, 1999. (Sutton Images)
15. 75 years of F1: Sid Watkins, Karl-Heinz Zimmerman, Eddie Baker, Charlie Whiting.
16. Malaysia, 2000. First corner accident. (LAT)
17. Grand Prix Drivers' Gold Day, 2000. (Allsport)
18. Canada, 1997. Panis with medical teams. (Actionimages)
19. Belgium, 1998. (Sutton Images)
20. The Alchemist. (Formula One Management)

21. Spa, 1966. Jackie Stewart's three friends in ecstasy. (Jock McDonald)
22. Nürburgring, 1968. JYS wins by over four minutes. (LAT)
23. Damon Hill, Champion 1996. (Allsport)
24. Graham Hill, World Champion 1962, 1988. (Allsport/ Hulton Deutsch)
25. Jim Clark, Champion 1963, 1965. (LAT)
26. Sir Stirling Moss. (Allsport)
27. Phil Hill, Champion 1961. (LAT)
28. Fangio, Le Mans. (Hulton Getty)
29. Innes Ireland, Watkins Glen, 1961. (LAT)
30. Jack Brabham, thrice champion. (LAT)
31. The man in the white suit. (Allsport)